Drawing
and
Perceiving

Second Edition

Douglas Cooper

VAN NOSTRAND REINHOLD
New York

Library of Congress Catalogue Card Number 91-33115
ISBN 0-442-00994-1

Printed in the United States of America

Van Nostrand Reinhold
115 Fifth Avenue
New York, New York 10003

Chapman and Hall
2-6 Boundary Row
London SE1 8HN, England

Thomas Nelson Australia
102 Dodds Street
South Melbourne 3205
Victoria, Australia

Nelson Canada
1120 Birchmount Road
Scarborough, Ontario MIK 5G4, Canada

16 15 14 13 12 11 10 9 8 7 6 5 4 3 2 1

Library of Congress Cataloging-in- Publication Data

Cooper, Douglas, 1946-
        Drawing and perceiving / Douglas Cooper—2nd ed.
            p.   cm.
        Includes bibliographical references and index.
        ISBN 0-442-00994-1
        1. Architectural drawing—Technique. 2. Visual Perception.
I. Title.
NA2708. C66, 1992   91-33115
720 ' . 28 ' 4—dc20   CIP

Contents

Preface

BACKGROUND, OVERVIEW, AND ACKNOWLEDGMENT OF SOURCES

This book has evolved from a drawing course I have taught to first-year architecture students at Carnegie Mellon University in Pittsburgh. Within that program, this was the only course in drawing these students would likely take during their studies or throughout their careers. Consequently, this introductory text has a long-term and comprehensive horizon extending well beyond the duration of that course. It presents the knowledge and experience of freehand and constructed drawing that are necessary both as a grounding for beginning students of architecture and design and as a continuing source of information for a lifetime in practice. Appropriate to its visual subject, this book presents through demonstration, and its format is that of an annotated picture book. It is hoped that this book will serve as that one book on drawing that architects and designers could buy if they would have only one book on the subject.

This book is also an alternative to some currently fashionable views on drawing, particularly those that have based their drawing pedagogy on the so-called left-brain, right-brain split. While I admire the student results that accompany the presentations of this point of view, I find the attribution of their success to be simplistic and limiting. That attribution emphasizes the powers of visualization of the right hemisphere and eschews any contribution from the left. More importantly for its effect, this explanation legitimizes a view that drawing ability relies solely on unfettered visual intuition.

If this book, therefore, has any overarching attitude toward drawing, then it would be that drawing is learned with the whole brain and not with a half brain. Yes, this book does call upon powers of visualization —from wherever in the brain these may arise. But, in developing drawing upon a kinesthetic foundation and against a background of multiple understandings of perception and in presenting material for the intellect as well as for the spirit, it also draws on powers of imitation, analysis, and rational thought.

A central contention of this text is that drawing is fundamentally a tactile and kinesthetic act. This point of view, which could be related to the transactionalist view of perception,[1] is presented in the first chapter, "The Shape of the Visual World." This chapter uses figure-drawing and the application of figure-drawing techniques to drawings of buildings to present drawing as a process of intense interaction with the visual world. My own introduction to this point of view owes to the drawing teacher Kimon Nicholaides, from whose book, *The Natural Way to Draw*, the exercises of the first section have been adapted and interpreted. My persistence with this point of view owes to my sense of its appropriateness to the task of architects and designers. Unlike painters, architects and designers must create something that does not yet exist before them. Whereas under many conditions the work of the painter might legitimately remain focused upon the reception and interpretation of sensation from the visual world, the work of the architect and designer must be directed squarely at the task of constructing that which is to be made visible in the world. Consistent with this aim, the exercises of this first section have a proactive character. They present the act of drawing as an *act of making* rather than as an act of viewing. This theme emerges as a general theme of the book and is developed in subsequent chapters as well.

The book's second chapter, "The Appearance of the Visual World," rests on the early work of the perceptual psychologist, James J. Gibson, one of the most articulate proponents of the ecological view of the question of perception. Since it is a central tenant of that point of view that sensation is in itself already ordered, Gibson's work is of particular use to architects and designers, who, as a matter of course, must assume the prospect of order. In general, the projects and exercises of this chapter have an analytical character. They are aimed at building knowledge of the order of the visual world as it exists and an understanding of drawing as a reasoned response to that order. Subjects covered in this section are *surface texture* (built on Gibson's understandings of textural gradient), *freehand perspective* (built on Gibson's understanding of depth cues), and studies into the re-ciprocal interactions of light, material, and form.

The third chapter, "Beyond Appearance," is more speculative. It uses my own work and that of children to develop the recurring theme of *drawing as making objects* (as against making appearances) and to state a position on the general question of *why* we make drawings. This work originated in an assignment given to me as a student in a first year drawing class taught by Professor Kent Bloomer, now of Yale University. Interpretations of the meaning of that original assignment and its subsequent work draw much from the writings of E. H. Gombrich.

The fourth chapter, "Conventions of Constuction," forms a reference on the conventions used by architects and designers. It presents their techniques of construction and discusses their uses and implications. This chapter is introduced with an essay on the importance of scaled documents to the design process. Using cognitive strategies of painting by analogy, it investigates reasons why architects and designers use drawings in the first place and shows the ways in which scaled representations empower and control the process of design itself.

During the years in which I have taught this course, I have had the privilege of working with many able colleagues and students. Acknowledging the substantial debt this work owes to these individuals would create a list too long for this volume, but I would like to mention a few. Professor John Pekruhn, who was the senior instructor of the course when I first came to Carnegie Mellon University, along with Robert Skydell, who assisted during the first two years, provided much-needed advice during my early years with the course. Paul Ostergaard, Raymond "Bud" Mall (some of whose photographs appear in this volume), Andrew Tesoro, and John Ritzu were important in the implementation of the exercises in the book's first and second chapters. More recently Janice Hart, Jim Quinnan, and Barry Shields have taught freehand drawing and watercolor, and Dana Buntrock, Mark English, Bruce Lindsey, Laura Nettleton, Paul Rosenblatt, and Nino Saggio have taught freehand drawing and perspective. In completing this revised version, Rebecca Schultz has provided much appreciated help in editing and provided several beautiful illustations.

Of all people, this book owes its greatest debt to Professor Kent Bloomer of Yale University. The assignments, criticism, and encouragement of that great educator originally led to my interest in drawing and its uses in architecture and design.

---

[1] A view of perception that emphasizes the role of interaction with the environment as a basis for perception. Leading proponents of this point of view are Adelbert Ames and John Dewey.

1
The Shape
of the
Visual World

A Tactile and Kinesthetic
Foundation Based on the Work
of Kimon Nicholaides

A TACTILE AND KINESTHETIC BASIS FOR DRAWING

Suspicions about Vision

It is an adage of hunting that a bird in the hand is worth two in the bush. While these words are largely directed at the uncertainties of marksmanship, they also hint at the vagaries of vision unaided by the affirming sense of touch. Likewise, when in some blissful moment we are wont to say, "Touch me, prove I'm not dreaming," we do so in recognition that it is through the sense of touch that we come closest to verification of the realness of things and events. Suspicions about vision originate in our understanding that, despite its obvious usefulness, vision may be considerably less essential than our other senses, most notably among them the sense of touch. Imagine a world without sight, and we are impressed by the prospect of the difficulty of everyday life. Imagine a world without touch, and we must wonder if life would be demonstrable or even possible.

What is so useful about vision is that it provides information at a distance. The unfolding image of an approaching car offers sufficient warning in itself, warning that is sufficient without the confirmation that would be provided by remaining in the middle of the road. Thus vision allows for a certain useful detachment from life, at more than arm's length and out of harm's way. But it is precisely for its capacity of detachment that we must consider vision as a kind of surrogate sense, a surrogate for its more fundamental relative, the sense of touch.

Consideration of vision as provider of a surrogate reality has been made amply evident by much of the televised reporting of the recent war in the Persian Gulf. I refer here to those chilling and riveting videos tracking smart bombs to their targets with the droll accompaniment of voice-over commentary. Our sense of detachment (and thus both our fascination and horror) was so complete that, as we watched, we also lost any sense of the human beings occupying the target or of the pain and destruction inflicted upon them. From the comfort of the living room, our perception remained confined to the visible, free of touch, and free of pain. To reverse for a moment a phrase from the 1980s, we had all of the gain (if one could call it that) and none of the pain.

If only because it is so easily deceived, there is ample cause to distrust the primacy of vision. Camouflage in warfare, trompe l'oeil in painting, and accelerated perspective in architecture and stage set design are all examples of the relative ease with which the eye can be fooled. What is instructive for our purposes is the fact that all of the above tricks unravel and fail in the moment the viewer can move freely while looking.

Among some perceptual psychologists, vision is understood as founded upon the sense of touch. The transactionalist position[1] by implication has given particular emphasis to the roles that touch and movement have as the basis for the other senses. According to this position, all perception is learned through a process of interaction (transaction) with the environment. In their view, the baby learns to see after verifying the visual field through much kicking, grasping, and moving about; the hitter in baseball learns to see a curve ball through much swinging (and missing); and the drawing student learns to see the world in perspective by first making lines converge to common vanishing points.

Vision Insufficient as a Basis for Drawing

If vision alone is an insufficient basis for the perceptions of daily life, is vision by itself equally suspect as a foundation for learning to draw? My own understanding of the limitations of vision as a singular basis for teaching drawing originated in a review I was conducting of the early results of the course featured in this book. After three years of teaching drawing to students of architecture, I felt I had seen a broad enough sample of the subsequent work of my former students to be able to assess the overall direction of my coursework. The results had been decidedly mixed. Many of my former students had been able to use their drawing ability as a design tool in subsequent studios, but many others, including some who during the first-year drawing course had seemed to draw well, had experienced great difficulty in transferring these abilities to their other coursework. Their difficulties were evident in drawings across the full range of the design process but were particularly obvious in their early generational drawings.

By chance it happened that I was reading a book about drawing, *The Natural Way to Draw* by Kimon Nicholaides,[2] at the same time I was conducting this review. Reading this book sharpened a long-standing suspicion of mine regarding an underlying cause of my students' problems. Earlier I had observed that the drawings of those who had encountered subsequent difficulty had lacked a quality that seemed evident in the drawings of those who had not; namely, their drawings seemed inactive and purely visual, whereas those of their more successful colleagues, though often less skillful, seemed active, gestural, rough, tactile, and even hewn by comparison. It occurred to me that a focus on the visual aspects of drawing at the expense of a kinesthetic and tactile foundation could be a contributing factor to the subsequent inability to use drawing effectively as a design tool.

Much of what Nicholaides wrote in introducing the exercises seemed to indicate a deep distrust of vision. In reading his words, I was even left with an impression that he considered vision unaided by the sense of touch to be almost voyeuristic in its detachment from reality. At the very least, I noted that his exercises proceed to purely visual observation only after prior kinesthetic activity.

Why Nicholaides's Approach is Suitable

By acknowledging the primacy of the sense of touch, Nicholaides's exercises require intense physical involvement with the objects drawn. They proceed by framing the act of drawing in a manner that is physically analogous to the act of touching. When students draw contours, they begin by imagining that the pencil is actually touching the surface of the model; when they model surfaces, they begin by imagining that the charcoal is actually manipulating that surface.

For its relationship to the recurring theme of *drawing as making* (to be taken up in detail in chapter 3) the latter exercise is of great interest because of the exercise that precedes it. Before modeling the surface of the figure, students are asked to imagine building its mass by considering the marks made by the charcoal as equivalent to material. They proceed by starting at the core of the figure and building out mark upon mark about that core, until they reach the outer surface. In the end these drawings acquire a brooding, weighty character that has little visual equivalence to the appearance of the model they represent. They do not in fact *look like* the model, but they are *made like* the model, and this attribute points to the reason why Nicholaides's pedagogy is so well suited to the task of architects and designers.

Architects and designers must provide the basis for making something that does not yet exist. Whereas the work of the painter might legitimately remain concentrated upon the reception and interpretation of sensation from the visual world, that of the architect and designer must be directed squarely at the task of constructing that which would be made visible in the world.[3] Consistent with this aim, this exercise (and, to a less obvious degree, the others as well) presents the act of drawing as an act of making a thing rather than as an act of viewing that thing. For the architect or designer faced with the task of designing something that does not yet exist, no other approach would be possible. If trained to draw only that which is visible, how could one begin to draw when nothing is there to draw? What first mark could one make that could lead one from such a stupefying cul-de-sac?

Chapter 1

Appropriate to Nicholaides's emphasis on active investigation, chapter 1 begins with a discussion on the kinesthetic basis of contour. The sequence of exercises begins with making contour and proceeds to making mass and volume. In all of these exercises, understandings are initiated with the figure and proceed only thereafter to drawings of buildings and other inanimate objects.

---

[1] The transactionalist position emphasizes the role of perceptual experience as a basis of perception. Principal advocates of this position include Adelbert Ames and John Dewey.

[2] Kimon Nicholaides, *The Natural Way to Draw*, (Boston: Houghton Mifflin, 1941).

[3] The Impressionists would provide an instance of nearly total concentration upon visual sensation.

CONTOUR

It is through physical movement that we come to understand surface contour.[4] We perceive a surface by moving along, across, and around that surface. An ice skater perceives the flatness of a pond by skating on it. A runner perceives the hilliness of the earth by running on it.

The shape of a surface is perceived through the deformation encountered in crossing that surface. A flat surface does not deform movement. A round surface deforms movement evenly about a point. A faceted surface deforms movement abruptly (at corners). A road through a Nebraska landscape deforms movement in one manner; a road through a mountainous landscape deforms movement in another manner.

Figure 1. *Nebraska Landscape.* A road through a Nebraska landscape deforms movement in one manner.

Figure 2. *Mountain Switchbacks.* A road through a mountainous landscape deforms movement in another manner.

---

[4] The term *contour* is used here to mean both outside contour or profile and cross-contour as it might be understood in cartography or in a usage such as *contour farming.*

Likewise, the quality of a surface is perceived through the deformation encountered in crossing that surface. The smoothness of silk and the roughness of muslin are both perceived by running one's fingers across their surfaces. Rough and smooth are both characteristics of crossing. We perceive that the puddles pictured at left are smooth, which is to say we recognize that we might slip in crossing them. We perceive that the river pictured at left is rough, which is to say we recognize that we might be swept away and drowned in crossing it.

Figure 3. *Smooth Puddles. Smooth* means smoothness of crossing: we might slip. Photo: Raymond Mall.

Figure 4. *Rough White Water. Rough* means roughness of crossing: we might drown. Photo: Raymond Mall.

CONTOUR

The shape of a surface can also be perceived through surrogates for our own movement. The material of which a surface is made is one such surrogate. In the case of objects with a high degree of material texture, the deformation of surface material patterns provides information sufficient to perceive their surface shape. We perceive the roundness of the neck of the wart hog pictured at right on the basis of the roundness of the pattern of creases on its neck; we perceive the roundness of the basket shown to the right on the basis of the roundness of the pattern of the reeds from which it is made.

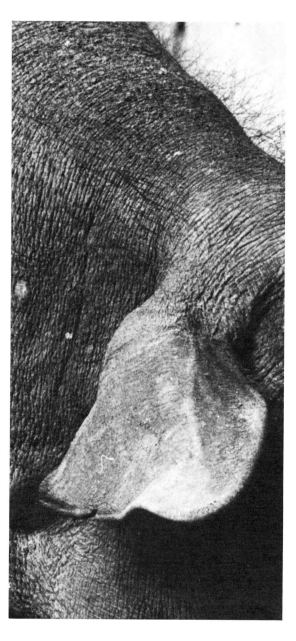

Figure 5. *Ear, Head, and Neck of a Wart Hog.* The deformation of the creases in the skin shows the roundness of the shape of the neck. Photo: Raymond Mall.

Figure 6. *Reed Basket.* The deformation of the reeds shows the roundness of the basket.

Whenever shape, through material deformation, is difficult to perceive or remains otherwise subsensory, existing material patterns may be emphasized or additional materials may be added to make shape more readable. The roundness of the wall shown at left is made more legible by the emphasis of material texture provided by the shadow cast by the rusticated courses of stone; the graceful shapeliness of a dancer's legs is made more apparent by wearing net stockings. The intention of shape articulation is one of the roots of decoration.[5]

Figure 7. *Stone Wall.* The deformation of the shadows cast by the rusticated courses of stone emphasizes the rounded shape of the wall.

Figure 8. *Fishnet Stockings.* Shape can be made more readable by the addition of more perceivable materials. Photo: Raymond Mall.

---

[5] It could be argued that such materials in today's market as wallpaper for interior walls and printed wood for appliances, which are anathema to contemporary architects and designers but so popular among the general public, may be so popular precisely because they compensate for a distinct lack of inherent material texture in today's building techniques and materials. The general population may be telling us that homogeneity is a problem.

CONTOUR
Exercise 1
Pure Following

Look at some point along the contour of the model, and, at the same time, imagine that your pen on the page is actually touching that point on the model at which you are looking.

Let your eyes slowly move along the contour of the model. Then, *without looking at your page* and in one continuous line, let your pen follow the movement of your eyes as they follow the contour over and across the surface of that model. As you draw, keep believing that your pen is, in fact, touching the model.[6]

Materials: Felt-tipped pen, bond paper.

Figure 9. Cynthia Sandling.

---

[6] Adapted from "Contour," in Kimon Nicholaides, *The Natural Way to Draw,* pp. 9-14.

Exercise 2
Modified Following

Draw the contour of the model as you did in
exercise 1, only in this instance glance occasionally at your page while you draw.[7]

Materials: Felt-tipped pen, bond paper.

Figure 10. Jo Frost.

---

[7] Adapted from " Contour," in Kimon Nicholaides, *The
Natural Way to Draw,* pp. 9-14.

CONTOUR
Exercise 3
Wrapping

Look at some point along the edge of the model. Hold your pen loosely on the paper. Keep looking at the model. Convince yourself that your pen on the page is touching that point on the model at which you are looking. Imagine that starting from that point on the figure you would wrap an endless ball of string around and around the model.

Let your eyes follow the path of that imagined wrapping. Let your pen follow the path of your eyes as they follow the path of the wrapping string.[8]

Materials: Felt-tipped pen, bond paper.

Figure 11. R. James Pett.
Figure 12. Marybeth Barrett.
Figure 13. (opposite page) Lawrence Qamar.
Figure 14. (opposite page) Paul Shea.

---

[8] Adapted from "Cross Contours," in Kimon Nicholaides, *The Natural Way to Draw,* pp. 20-22.

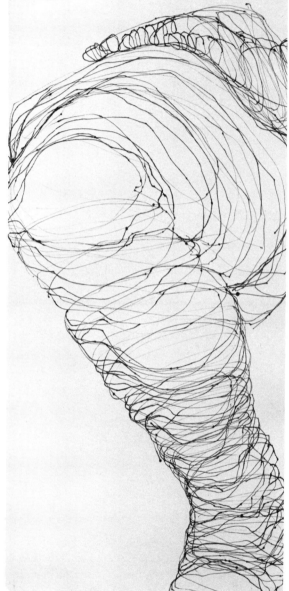

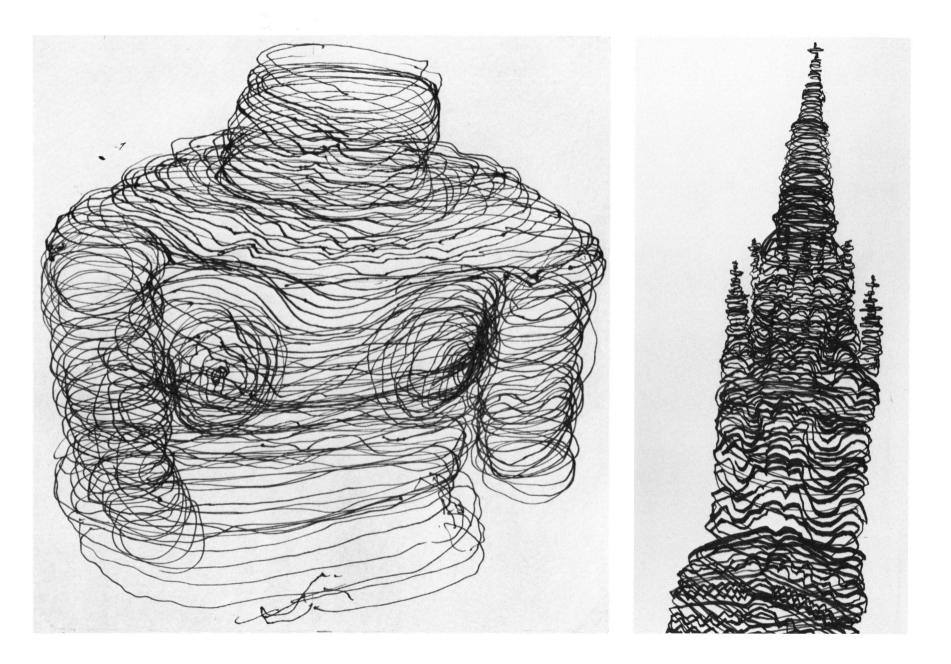

11

CONTOUR
Exercise 4
Half-Wrapping

Imagine wrapping the model just as you did
in the previous exercise, *Wrapping,* but this
time show only that part of the wrapping that
would be visible.[9]

Materials: Felt-tipped pen, bond paper.

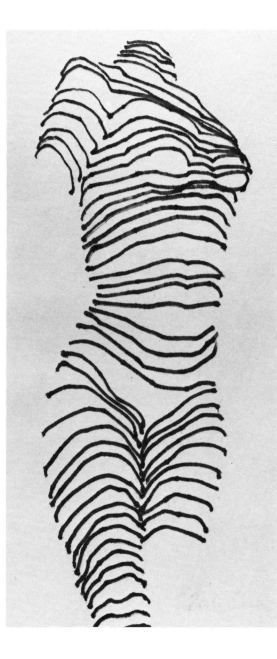

Figure 15. Paul Shea.
Figure 16. Mark Dininno.
Figure 17. (opposite page) Richard Schmitz.
Figure 18. (opposite page) Scott Fisher.

[9] Adapted from "Cross Contours," in Kimon Nicholaides,
The Natural Way to Draw, pp. 20-22.

13

GESTURE

The form of motionless objects is a consequence of force. Their lack of motion indicates only that the present forces are counterbalanced; it does not indicate a lack of force. We are able to perceive forces present in motionless objects. We describe posture with words such as *crouch, slouch,* or *lean,* words that describe our perception of the muscular resolution of each stance. We see a poised cat or a coiled snake and feel the intense balance of forces despite the stillness of the animal.

The intent of gesture is to give form to these perceptions. It does so through empathetic[10] sensation, literally, by drawing a thing, feeling the same sensations as that thing.

Figure 19. *Eiffel as the Tower* (after a drawing from *Punch,* 1889). Empathetic sensation is feeling the same sensations as another thing.

---

[10] *Empathy* is usually used to mean a capacity to share the emotional feelings of another person. It is used here by analogy to mean a capacity to share the physical sensation of another person or, by transfer, of an inanimate thing.

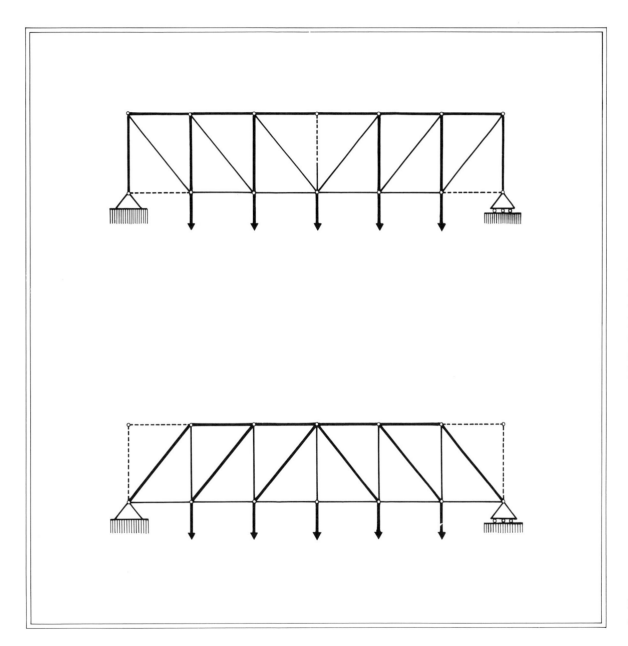

In a sense, the intent of gesture drawing, particularly as it is applied to buildings, is similar to the intent of an analysis of forces in a course in statics. Though the two activities are obviously different (one is qualitative, intuitive, and instantaneous, whereas the other is quantitative, methodical, and time-consuming), both do share a common fundamental goal: understanding the resolution of the forces of a structure. In that sense, gesture could be called intuitive statics.

Of all of the elements of drawing, gesture is the most important. In a sense, no drawing can possibly escape the dominance of gesture. Each drawing is, after all, recorded gesture. At its barest, a drawing is gesture's past tense: that which was gestured. Nevertheless, the primacy of gesture must be constantly kept in mind; without an underlying sense of gesture, a drawing, however competent it might be in other respects, is dead.

Figure 20. *Analysis of Forces in Two Trusses.* Gesture drawing might be called intuitive statics.

15

GESTURE
Exercise 1

The model will take a series of quick, active poses that will last between twenty seconds and one minute.

As the model holds the pose, let your crayon sweep freely and continuously around the paper. Your hand should move rapidly and be driven by a sense of the forces present in the pose. Where an arm droops, let your lines also droop. Where a foot is pushing off a floor, let your lines also push off a floor.

You should not try to draw the appearance of the model. Rather, try to draw the activity of the model. Your hand and your lines should do what the model is doing. To this end, it is generally wise to avoid fixing on one visual attribute, for example, contour.[11]

Materials: Lithographic crayon or charcoal, newsprint.

Figure 21. Jean Geiger and Albert Kim.

---

[11] Adapted from "Gesture," in Kimon Nicholaides, *The Natural Way to Draw,* pp. 14-20.

Exercise 2

Poses by the model and slide views of buildings will be alternated. Draw gesture drawings of both. As you draw, try to transfer the ease with which you draw from the figure to your drawing from buildings.[12]

Materials: Lithographic crayon or charcoal, newsprint.

Figure 22. Rebecca Schultz.

[12] Adapted from "Gesture," in Kimon Nicholaides, *The Natural Way to Draw,* pp. 14-20.

17

MASS AND VOLUME

The most basic knowledge we can have about our surroundings is that something is out there or that nothing is out there. We can make two distinctions about the out there:[13] 1) how far out from us the *something* or *nothing* is or extends and 2) in what direction out from us the *something* is or extends.

Let us approach the out there as if we were blind: The *something out there* is whatever we might bump into or have bump into us. It is solid. It is where we are unable to go. In the plan at right, it is the solid buildings (shown in black) of the city of Siena. The *nothing out there* is wherever we might go without bumping into something or having something bump into us. It is empty space. It is where we are able to go. In the plan at right, it is the streets and piazzas (shown in white) between the buildings of Siena and the empty space surrounding the city.

Figure 23. *Plan of Siena.* Empty space is where we can go. The solid is where we cannot go.

---

[13] The phrase "the out there" is from Delbert Highlands, "Translation," in *Representation and Architecture*, ed. Omer Akin and Eleanor Weinel (Silver Spring, Md.: Information Dynamics, 1982) pp. 237-243.

Of the two parts, the solid and the empty space, we can sense only the solid. Only solids provide sensation. Solids resist deformation; empty space does not. Solids hurt; empty space does not. Solids reciprocate, and their reciprocation provides us with the sensory matter with which we construct our perception of their existence and their form.

Figure 24. *Radar View of the Normandy Beaches on D-Day.* The view records the solids, not the empty space. The position of the airplane (in this case, the viewer) is indicated by the bright spot in the middle. The invasion fleet is visible massed off the coast.

MASS AND VOLUME

The shapes and sizes of solids and volumes are perceived through the sensations of our interaction with them. To perceive their shape is to recognize form in a movement against, across, along, or around a solid. To perceive spiral, as in the example to the right, is to recognize the constantly increasing or decreasing radius of curvature within a movement about and along an axis. To perceive size is to understand the measure of a movement (with respect to one's own body) across, along, or around a solid. To perceive that Russia is wide is to recognize that it takes a long time to cross.

Figure 25. *Spirals*. A spiral is a form of movement about a solid.

Solids are perceived as constructs of the sensations they provide to us. Regular and irregular solids are perceived as continua of regular or irregular resistance to deformation by forces that we apply directly, such as pushing and pulling, or to forces applied by trustable substitutes, such as light, sound, wind, and thrown objects. A cube resists deformation in a manner characteristic of cubes; a sphere resists deformation in a manner characteristic of spheres.

Figure 26. *Column at the Edge of a Portal.* Solids are perceived as continua of regular or irregular resistance. Drawing: Rebecca Schultz.

MASS AND VOLUME

Except through the agency of solids, empty space cannot be perceived. Where, through the agency of solids, it can be perceived, empty space becomes a thing in its own right: a volume.

Volumes can be perceived only where they can be recognized either by association to a solid, as its inverse, or by implication of a solid as its missing part. To perceive a square room is to recognize the inverse of a square solid. To perceive an opening is to recognize a missing part within a pattern of sensation characteristic to a wall. In the drawing to the right, for example, the cupola is perceived as the inverse of an eight-sided solid, and the crypt is perceived as a missing part within the rock beneath the church.

Figure 27. *Section through a Hilltop Church.* Volumes can be perceived either by association to or by implication of a solid.

Some volumes can be perceived both as the inverse of a solid and as the missing part of an incomplete solid. Such volumes are called *figural* volumes. The cupola in the drawing to the left, for example, can be perceived both as the inverse of a conical solid and as the missing part of the solid earth.

Figure 28. *Section through Termite Mounds and Cupolas.* Volumes that can be perceived as both the inverse of a solid and its missing part are called *figural* volumes.

MASS
Exercise 1
Massing with Lithographic Crayon

Position the lithographic crayon at the center of the page. Imagine that the crayon is positioned at the center of gravity of the model. Build mass out from that center: behind, below, to the sides, and in front of the center. Work as if packing layers of snow onto a snowball or layers of clay onto an armature. Keep building outward until you reach the surface of the model.

When it is completed, your drawing should be dark where the model is thick and light where the model is thin.[14]

Materials: Lithographic crayon, bond paper.

Figure 29. *Massing with Lithographic Crayon.* Christopher Farley.

---

[14] Adapted from "Weight," in Kimon Nicholaides, *The Natural Way to Draw,* pp. 33-35.

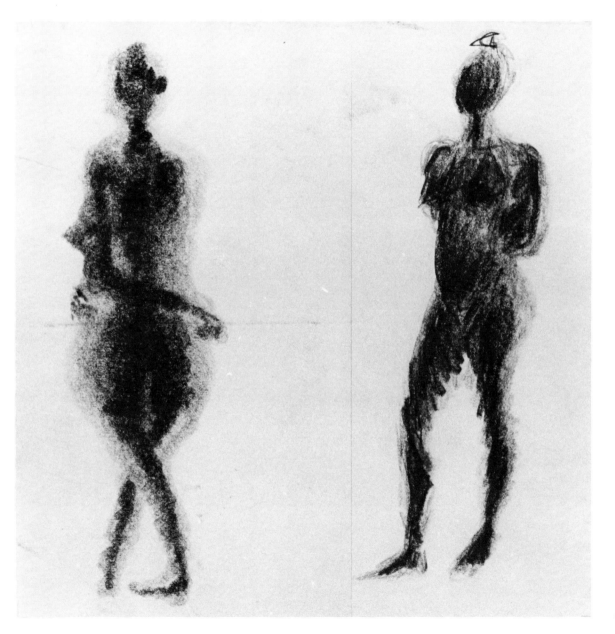

Exercise 2
Massing with Ink Scribble

Position the pen at the center of the page. Imagine that the pen is positioned at the center: behind, below, to the sides, and in front of the center. Work as if packing layers of snow onto a snowball or layers of clay onto an armature. Keep building outward until you reach the surface of the model.

When it is complete, your drawing should be dark where the model is thick and light where the model is thin.[15]

Materials: Felt-tipped pen, bond paper. (note: example to the left uses lithographic crayon)

Figure 30. *Massing with Lithographic Crayon.* Kevin Kertesz (left), Norma Barbacci (right).

[15] Adapted from "Weight," in Kimon Nicholaides, *The Natural Way to Draw,* pp. 33-36.

MASS
Exercise 3
Modeling with Charcoal

Lightly build out the mass of the figure with tone (as you did in exercises 1 and 2 but more rapidly and lightly). When you reach the surface of the figure, model that surface. Where the surface moves back away from you, press the charcoal into the page. Where the surface moves out toward you, ease the pressure on the charcoal.

Your drawing is the result of your imitating the movement of the surface in the manner of a relief. Your drawing is a mechanical record of the direction and force of your mimicry. Black means and results from pressing hard; gray means and results from pressing lightly.[16]

Materials: Charcoal (soft black), newsprint.

Figure 31. J. Andrés Petruscak.
Figure 32. (opposite page) Kimberly Ruane Biagioli.
Figure 33. (opposite page) David Barger.

---

[16] Adapted from "Modeled in Litho-Crayon," in Kimon Nicholaides, *The Natural Way to Draw*, pp. 36-39.

MASS
Exercise 4
Modeling with Ink Scribble

Lightly build out the mass of the figure with ink scribble (as you did in exercises 1 and 2 but more rapidly and lightly). When you reach the surface of the figure, model that surface. Where the surface moves back away from you, scribble more. Where the surface moves out toward you, scribble less.

As you do this exercise, think of sanding a piece of wood. Where you would want the form to go in, you would sand more. Where you would want the form to come out, you would sand less.[17]

Materials: Felt-tipped pen, newsprint.

Figure 34. Tammy Roy.
Figure 35. Lois J. Moore.
Figure 36. (opposite page) Rebecca Schultz.
Figure 37. (opposite page) Paul Shea.

---

[17] Adapted from "Modeled in Ink," in Kimon Nicholaides, *The Natural Way to Draw*, pp. 51-52.

MASS
Exercise 5
Modeling with Watercolor

Using ocher, lightly build out the mass of the figure with tone (as you did in exercises 1 and 2 but more rapidly and lightly). When you reach the surface of the figure, model that surface with umber wash. Where the surface moves back away from you, lay umber wash over the surface. Where the surface moves out toward you, leave the surface as ocher or, better still, as white space. (Leaving the surface as white space does require some preplanning.)

Compared to previous exercises using charcoal and ink, this exercise is more symbolic in its treatment of the act of modeling. Whereas the former presented a mechanical analogy to modeling (pressing in with charcoal corresponded mechanically to the act of actually pushing back the surface), this exercise represents this act with color. It is therefore important that, as you draw, you heighten your sense of the weight of the umber wash so as to imagine it depressing the page.[18]

Materials: Calligraphy brush, burnt umber watercolor, yellow ocher watercolor, watercolor paper (can be of low quality).

Figure 38. Katherine Ruffin.

---

[18] Adapted from "Modeled in Water Color," in Kimon Nicholaides, *The Natural Way to Draw*, pp. 68-70.

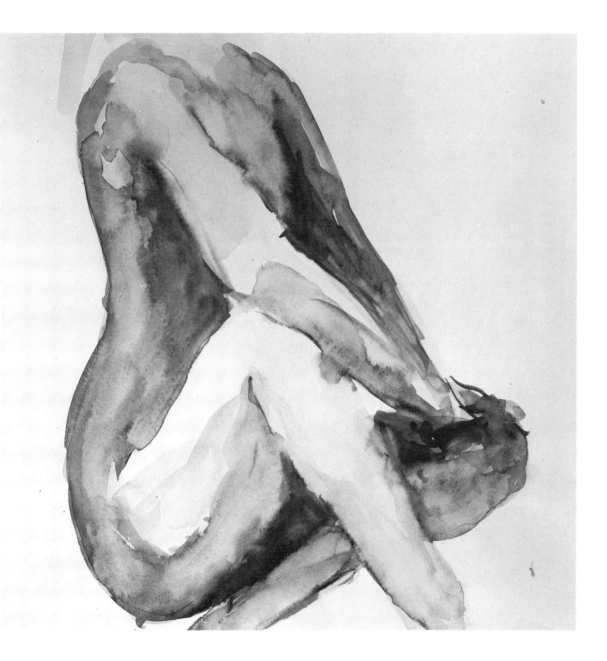

Exercise 6
Rapid Massing with Watercolor

More rapidly than in the previous exercise, use ocher to lightly build out the mass of the figure with tone. When you reach the surface of the figure, model that surface rapidly using umber wash. Where the surface moves back away from you, lay umber wash over the surface. Where the surface moves out toward you, leave the surface as ocher or, better still, as white space. (Leaving the surface as white space does require some preplanning.) Speed is of the utmost importance in doing this exercise; it should be done at a breakneck pace.[19]

Materials: Calligraphy brush, burnt umber watercolor, yellow ocher watercolor, watercolor paper (can be of low quality).

Figure 39. Rebecca Schultz.

[19] Adapted from "Modeled in Water Color," in Kimon Nicholaides, *The Natural Way to Draw*, pp. 68-70.

VOLUME
Exercise 1
Deep-Shallow

Construct a still life characterized by interesting and articulate voids. Then with brushed ink distinguish between deep (where the still life is not) and shallow (where the still life is). Where the *out there* is deep, brush in ink; where the *out there* is shallow, leave the paper blank.

As you draw, try to understand volume as the figural element of the composition. To this end it is helpful if you avoid generating the voids by drawing their outlines first. Though it is more difficult to do so, try instead to generate the voids outward from their centers.

Materials: India ink, calligraphy brush, bond paper.

Figure 40. Bill Birkholz.

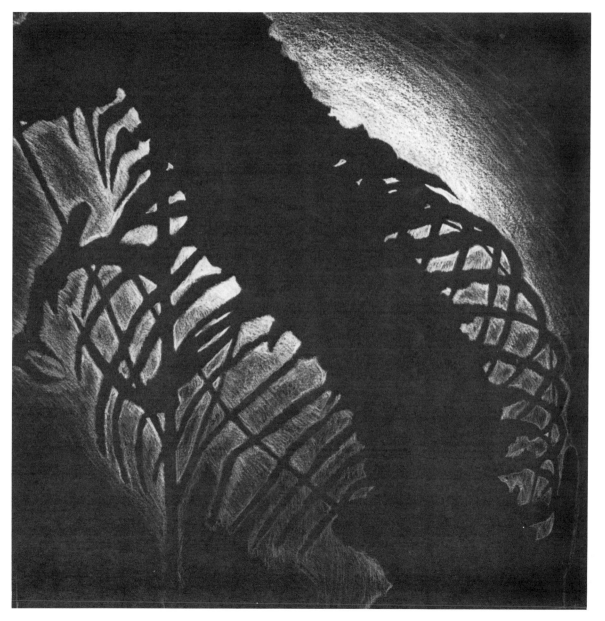

Exercise 2
Deep-Shallow

View a skeleton from a direction of sight that is characterized by interesting and articulate voids. Compose your view in a way that will be supportive of an understanding of volume as a figural element in your composition. Then, with white colored pencil, distinguish between deep (where the skeleton is not) and shallow (where the skeleton is). Where the *out there* is deep, draw; where the *out there* is shallow, leave the paper blank.

As you proceed, pay special attention to the marks on the paper. Try to make the marks contribute to a figural reading of volume. To this end, it is helpful if you avoid generating the voids by drawing their outlines first. Though it is more difficult to do so, try instead to generate the voids outward from their centers.

Materials: White Prismacolor, black construction paper.

Figure 41. Paul Martinchich.

VOLUME
Exercise 3
Deepest, Deeper, Deep
Shallow, Shallower, Shallowest.

Go to a deep forest or a plant conservatory. Choose a foliage array that is characterized by both significant and well-articulated depth and interesting and articulate voids; that is, the scene you choose should have clear layers of foliage that document several positions of depth.

Then, with Conté crayon or soft charcoal, distinguish between areas in the scene that are deepest, deeper, deep, and shallow, shallower, shallowest. Where the volume between you and the foliage is deeper, your drawing should become darker; where the volume between you and the foliage is shallower, your drawing should remain lighter. In the end, you should seek to achieve a murky and highly atmospheric sense of depth not unlike that of an extremely foggy day. As your drawing proceeds, you should understand volume as a figural element.

Materials: Conté crayon, newsprint.

Figure 42. Yong Lee.

34

Exercise 4
The Volume Between

Find a broad facade of a building that is characterized by openings of a variety of sizes (and shapes as well). Pick a diagonal view of the facade.

Then, with charcoal, describe the depth of the volume between you and the facade. Where the volume between you and the facade is deep, draw more; where the volume between you and the facade is shallow, draw less. As you draw, try to believe that you are making the atmosphere that fills the distance between you and the facade. Just as in the previous exercise, your drawing should achieve a character in which the volume has an almost material quality.

Materials: Charcoal (soft black), newsprint. (Instructor note: Facades used for this assignment must articulate sufficient depth. They should have deep openings and deep reveals.)

Figure 43. John Seitz.

35

VOLUME
Exercise 5
The Volume Within

Pick an architectural subject that is characterized by a dominant internal volume. A good subject might be a grouping of columns, such as the pulpit shown at right, the volume beneath a heavy and ornate table, or a large hall with multiple structural bays. If no architectural subject is available, a skeleton or an arrangement of bicycles would be suitable.

Then, with ink scribble or soft pencil, describe the subject in terms of the thickness of the volume within the void. In the sense that you strive to give the volume a material quality, you should draw as you did in the previous exercise, *The Volume Between.* In this instance, however, you should consciously try to occupy the internal volume with your pen or pencil while you draw.

Materials: Felt-tipped pen or Ebony pencil, newsprint.

Figure 44. Rebecca Schultz.
Figure 45. (opposite page) Rebecca Schultz.

36

2
The Appearance of the Visual World

A Foundation on the Underlying
Order of Appearances Based on
the Work of James J. Gibson

THE ORDER OF APPEARANCE

Gibson: The Ecological Point of View

With the foundation of Kimon Nicholaides's investigative exercises in the first chapter firmly established, we can now (and only now) proceed to an analytical approach to the question of appearance. While views on this question are numerous, this chapter refers to only one: the early work of the perceptual psychologist James J. Gibson.[1] Gibson, who has been one of the most articulate proponents of the so-called ecological view of perception, began his work during the early stages of World War II, when he was contracted by the United States government to help in the development of what might be best described as a forerunner of present-day flight simulators. At that time, a large number of pilot trainees were experiencing difficulty in surviving their early missions. In view of the cost in both men and machines, it was considered critical to gain a more precise understanding of the nature of the visual environment in which the pilots would have to function.

Beginning with this work, Gibson came to state a fundamentally new position with respect to the question of perception. While not entirely discounting the roles of predisposing schemata or perceptual learning that were central to the gestalt psychologists and transactionalists,[2] respectively, Gibson has argued that human perceptual systems are founded on an order that already exists in the environment around us. With respect to vision, Gibson has argued that the light that enters our eyes arrives in a state that is already structured by the planes and surfaces from which it has been reflected. To Gibson, the sensory data of the world already possess sufficient order such that perceiving can proceed on that data alone.

The importance of this point of view to students of architecture and design cannot be overestimated and goes beyond the fact that Gibson is most articulate in explaining phenomena that are complicated and in dispute. Of key importance is the aforementioned central tenant of the ecological point of view, namely, that sensation is, in itself, already ordered. The dangers of this stance not withstanding (it is essentially an absolutist argument), it provides the prospect of a general order in the visual world that is independent of relativist concerns, together with useful insights into the nature of spatial order, whatever its origins. These matters are of great importance to architects and designers, who, as a matter of course, must presume at least the possibility of a spatial order. What is the nature of the order that Gibson found in the visual environment?

Gibson and the Textural Gradient

Gibson found order in the visual texture of the material world. Beginning with his wartime investigations of flight conditions such as whiteout, Gibson came to believe that vision was dependent on the presence of surface texture. Whiteout is a condition affecting pilots who are flying through thick fog and who are no longer able to discern the ground surface or the contours of clouds. Under such conditions, which are often made all the more confusing by G-force alterations of gravitational orientation, pilots can become completely disoriented despite the presence of adequate illumination. Gibson traced the disorientation of these conditions to the absence of surface texture. Ultimately he reached the more general conclusion that visual texture alone was a sufficient condition for visual perception.[3]

To Gibson *visual texture* has been a broadly inclusive term. It includes textures of many characters, artificial as well as natural, whether floors of square tiles or lawns of blades of grass. It includes textures at multiple scales, whether fields of grain stalks or a rectangular patchwork of fields in Iowa. It includes textures of all sorts of shapes, whether rectangular bricks in walls or round beer barrels in rows. Gibson has found visual texture to be a natural condition of matter itself, matter that, by virtue of being made of discrete and repeated parts and by virtue of the geometry of ocular projection, would be projected into our eyes in an ordinal[4] and therefore visually coherent manner. Gibson has come to use the term *textural gradient* to describe this characteristic of the visual field, and he has used this term to explain the perception of common phenomena within the visual world. He explains the perception of frontal surfaces, longitudinal surfaces, corners, and edges on the basis of the characteristic textural gradient they project onto the retina. Frontal surfaces are understood as projecting uniform gradients, longitudinal surfaces (i.e., surfaces such as a floor that are more or less parallel to the line of sight) are understood as projecting gradients that diminish with greater distance from the observer, and both corners and edges are understood as projecting conditions that shift abruptly from one gradient to another. From this understanding of surface, Gibson has proceeded to build an understanding of depth.

Gibson and Depth Cues

Depth cues are conditions of the visual field such as overlap and perspective that commonly yield perceptions of depth. Though they had already been identified by others, Gibson's work has contributed much to furthering a basic understanding of depth cues. Whereas perceptions of surface attitude, corner, edge, and the like might be termed first-order characteristics of the visual field, the building blocks, so to speak, depth cues might be termed second-order characteristics. What stands out in Gibson's explanations of the depth cues is that, in a manner similar to his discussion of corners, edges, and the like, in explaining these, he also points to the characteristic signature of the information arising in the environment rather than to the input of any schemata or prior learning; that is, he relies on the characteristic optical array of textural gradients to explain how these function as cues.

Gibson breaks depth cues into two groups: primary cues and secondary cues. The first group is dependent upon the existence of two eyes or upon subtle sensations of muscular response. They are effective only within short distances from the observer. Because they are also involved with conditions of the observer and only to a lesser degree with the conditions of the environment, for the purposes of Gibson's central argument, they are the least interesting. These primary cues are:

1) *Accommodation:* the changing focal length at various distances from the observer.
2) *Disparity vision:* the disparity of the views between the two eyes.
3) *Convergence:* the angle at which eyes converge in focusing on objects at various distances.

The second group is more dependent on the information of the optical array. Except for the last of these, *motion parallax,* these cues are also more interesting for our purposes because they can be replicated in drawings. They might be more properly called the pictorial cues. I list them in the order in which, in my observation, they are acquired as conventions in making drawings. They are:

1) *Upward position in the visual field:* the tendency of objects, seen against a ground surface, to be positioned higher in the visual field with greater distance from the observer.
2) *Overlap:* the tendency of near objects to overlap far objects.
3) *Shade and shadow:* three dimensional modeling of objects in light, shade, and shadow.

4) *Size perspective:* the apparent reduction in size of objects of known size with greater distance from the observer.
5) *Aerial perspective:* the effect of air on the color and visual acuity of objects at various distances from the observer.
6) *Linear perspective:* the apparent convergence of parallel lines to common vanishing points with increasing distance from the observer.
7) *Motion parallax:* apparent relative motions of objects at various distances from an observer in motion.

Chapter 2

Chapter 2 begins with a pictorial essay on Gibson's understandings of textural gradient and the pictorial depth cues. Exercises that follow cover freehand perspective and rendition of light. In the spirit of Gibson, all of these are presented in the spirit of uncovering the order of the visual environment.

---

[1] James J. Gibson, *The Perception of the Visual World* (Boston: Houghton Mifflin Co., 1950) Chapters 1-9.
[2] Gestalt psychology: as applied to perceptual psychology, a view that emphasizes the role of predisposing laws that govern the configuration of form. Transactional psychology: a view of perception that emphasizes the role of interaction with the environment as a basis for perception.
[3] Gibson modified his view in two subsequent books. *The Senses Considered as Perceptual Systems* emphasized the contribution of kinesthetic interaction with the environment and the interaction of the senses with each other. *The Ecological Approach to Visual Perception* emphasized *motion parallax* as the key feature of the optical array.
[4] Having ordered intervals between stimuli.

SURFACE TEXTURE

According to Gibson, the fundamental condition for the perception of a surface is that
the surface has texture. Only surfaces with
texture can be focused on the retina. It is
impossible to form an optical image of a
completely smooth surface, for example, a
mirror.

Surface texture is projected onto the retina in
an ordinal way corresponding to the texture's
material character (fine or course), its shape
(flat or round), its attitude relative to the
observer (frontal or longitudinal), and its
distance from the observer (larger if near,
smaller if far); that is to say, the light reflected
from a surface onto the retina projects an
array of stimuli that corresponds (and is
therefore readable) both to the nature of that
surface and to its position relative to the
observer.

Figure 46. *Wood Texture*. Only surfaces having texture can
be focused on the retina. Surface texture is projected to the
retina in an ordinal way. Photo: Raymond Mall.

Surface texture is a broadly inclusive term. It includes textures of many characters, manufactured as well as natural: floors of gridded tiles or lawns of blades of grass. It includes textures at multiple scales: fields of grain stalks or a patchwork of fields in a Midwest landscape. In the example at left, legible texture is found at the scale of the building part (the crenelations at the top of the gable and the regular and repeated window openings within the turret), at the scale of material (the individual stones), and at the scale of the architectural detail (the patterned decorative carving around the window).

Figure 47. *Stone Turret.* Surface texture exists at multiple scales.

SURFACE TEXTURE

Figure 48. *Liberty Center, Pittsburgh, Pa.* Burt Hill Kosar Rittelmann Associates, The Architects Collaborative, UDA Architects. Perception of a flat frontal surface.

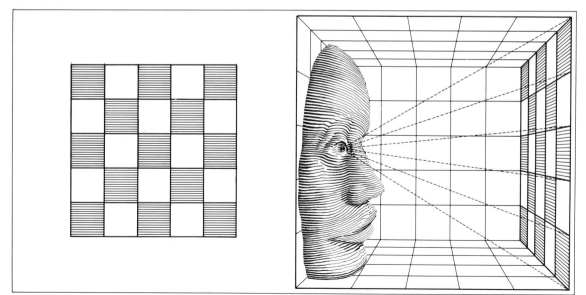

Perception of a flat frontal surface A flat frontal surface projects an array of stimuli onto the retina whose gradient (interval between stimuli) is constant. Figure 49.

Figure 50. *Street Paving.* Perception of a flat longitudinal surface. Photo: Raymond Mall.

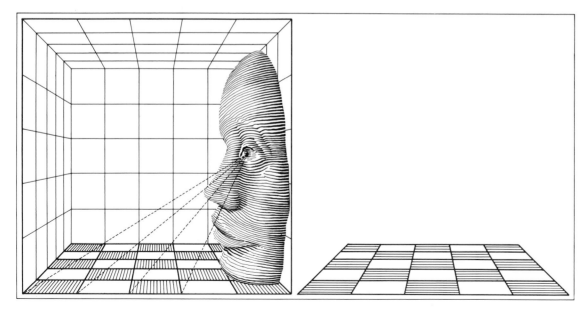

Perception of a flat longitudinal surface A flat longitudinal surface projects an array of stimuli onto the retina, whose gradient decreases and nears the center of the retina with increasing distance from the observer.
Figure 51.

SURFACE TEXTURE

Figure 52. *Awnings and roofs above Kennywood Park.*
Perception of a flat slanting surface.

Perception of a flat slanting surface A flat slanting surface projects an array of stimuli onto the retina, whose gradient decreases and nears the center of the retina either more or less rapidly than that of a longitudinal surface. Figure 53.

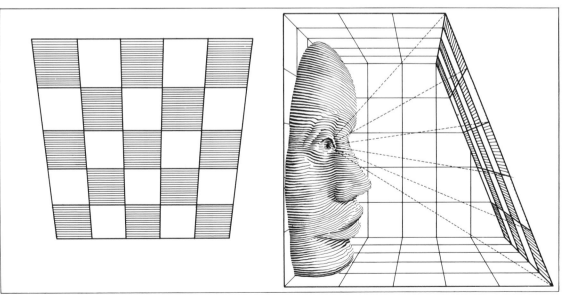

Figure 54. *Three Rivers Stadium.* Perception of a rounded surface.

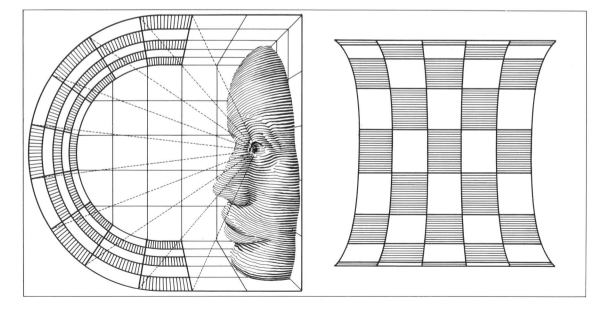

Perception of a rounded surface A rounded surface projects an array of stimuli onto the retina, whose gradient changes from small to large to small as the surface curves from a longitudinal to a frontal and back to a longitudinal attitude relative to the observer. Figure 55.

47

SURFACE TEXTURE

Figure 56. *Liberty Center, Pittsburgh, Pa.* Burt Hill Kosar Rittelmann Associates, The Architects Collaborative, UDA Architects. Perception of a Corner

Perception of a corner A corner of a surface projects an array of stimuli onto the retina, whose gradient abruptly shifts from one corresponding to that surface in one attitude to one corresponding to that surface in another attitude. Figure 57.

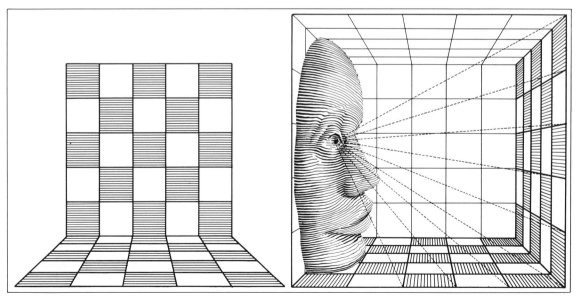

48

Figure 58. *Three Buildings.* Perception of an Edge.

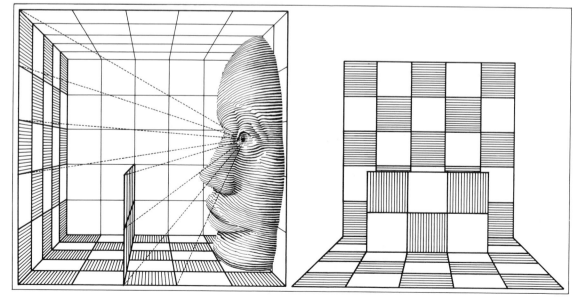

Perception of an edge An edge of a surface projects an array of stimuli onto the retina, whose gradient abruptly shifts from one corresponding to that surface to one corresponding to the surface of a background. Figure 59.

49

SURFACE TEXTURE
Exercise 1
Deformed Surface Pattern [5]

According to Gibson, the presence of adequate illumination is insufficient as a basis for perception. In his view, form can be perceived on the basis of surface texture alone. The following exercise rests on this understanding.

Select a piece of cloth (or other woven material) that has a uniform pattern (such as stripes or a plaid) either woven into or printed onto its surface. Arrange the cloth so that a series of interesting folds are created and so that the arrangement of the cloth can be inferred solely as a function of the deformation of the regular pattern. Then draw the pattern. Draw only the pattern. Do *not* draw the outlines of the cloth or the folds, except as they may be parts of the deformation of the pattern itself. Do *not* describe the variation of light on the surface.

Materials: Soft pencil, bond paper, printed cloth or other woven material.

Figure 60. David McKee.

[5] Assignment from Professor Randall Korman, Syracuse University.

Exercise 2
Profile, Materiality, and Surface Texture

Objects in nature possess surface texture as a natural condition of their manner of formation or growth. Among things as diverse as horns of sheep with their annular rings, pineapples with their diamond-patterned surface, and limestone cliffs with their layers of sediment, we understand surface form in large measure as a variant of these formation textures. Likewise, Gibson explains the phenomenon of edges or profile on the basis of sudden shifts of such textures, from one corresponding to the overlapping material to one corresponding to the background material. The following exercise builds understanding of the contributions of texture to both form and profile.

Select at least three objects of various forms, materials, and textures. Use as many objects as you wish, but at least one object should be organic. Draw the arrangement as an array of various surface textures. Pay careful attention to the characteristic textures of the individual materials as well as to the ways in which these textures deform with variations of shape.

Materials: Soft pencil or carbon pencil, charcoal paper, at least three objects (one organic) of various surface textures.

Figure 61. David McKee.

SURFACE TEXTURE
Exercise 3
Surface and Distance of View [6]

Thus far, owing to the sizes of the drawings relative to the sizes of the originals, the material textures we have drawn were presented at a size (both in the original and the drawing) at which we could feel fairly confident that what we were drawing was the actual material of the object. But it is often the case in drawing that material textures are subsensory, or constraints of size prohibit their one-to-one representation. In such cases, drawn textures are invented as substitutes for the true material textures of the object. While these substitute textures must share certain formal properties with the original, they do not necessarily represent textures that are physically present on the original. The engraver of a dollar bill does not, after all, believe that Washington's face was covered with horizontal stripes. Rather, these stripes indicate how Washington's face would appear if it were made of stripes, and on this conditional basis we are still able to perceive form, in this case his face.

The exercise that follows raises a similar problem of inventing surface texture, but in this case it operates by enlarging the size of what is shown to a point that exceeds our ability to perceive supporting textural information in the original. Particularly in the

---

[6] Assignment adapted from an assignment from Professor Delbert Highlands, Carnegie Mellon University.

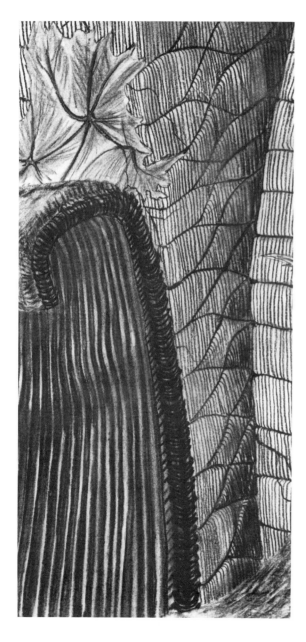

case of drawing the nearer views of this assignment, you will be put in the position of having to invent the textures you are drawing.

Select two kinds of food of contrasting surface texture such as meat and bread or butter and crackers. Arrange them so that one object overlaps the other. Then draw a series of views describing an approach toward a point along the overlapping edge. Keep drawing views until you reach a view in which the identity of the original foods is no longer discernible.[7]

Materials: Charcoal or Conté crayon, charcoal paper.

Figures 62, 63, 64, and 65. Paul Shea.

---

[7] As an extension of this exercise, try the following: After having reached the point at which the identities of the materials are lost, redefine the two materials. Then draw a series of views describing a withdrawal from the overlapping edge between these two new materials. In effect, you will have transformed the original materials into two new materials through a process of analysis, a process of breaking a material into its constituent parts.

SURFACE TEXTURE
Project 1
Organic Form

This project aims at uniting the earlier studies in this chapter on material textures with some initial indications of variation of light on surfaces. The primary medium will be charcoal, and the study will include a range of both fragmentary sketches and completed drawings.

The project will begin with the theme of forms that grow lengthwise. Subjects include animal horns, hooves, and teeth, as well as branches of trees. Later themes will be material, surface, and light; subjects for these studies will be wood, fur, skin, feathers, scales, etc. The overall aim of this project is to gain knowledge of various materials as they are perceived in various conditions of light and as they are perceived in the guise of various shapes.

Figure 66. Jeffrey Pitchford.
Figure 67. (opposite page) David McKee.
Figure 68. (opposite page) Scot Wallace.

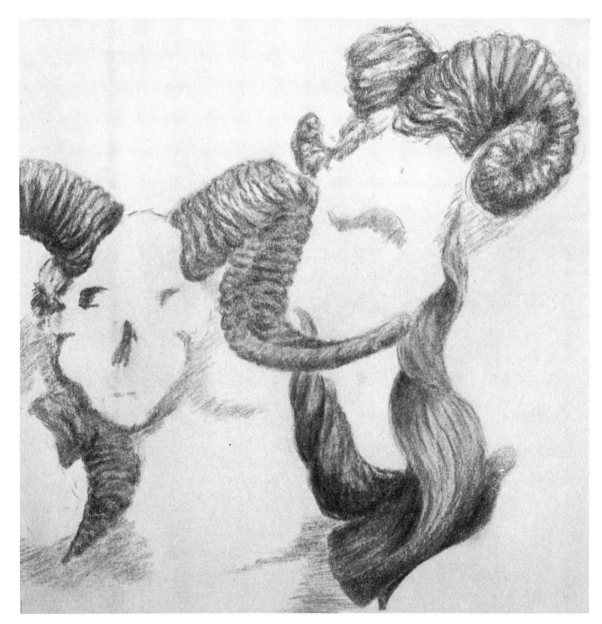

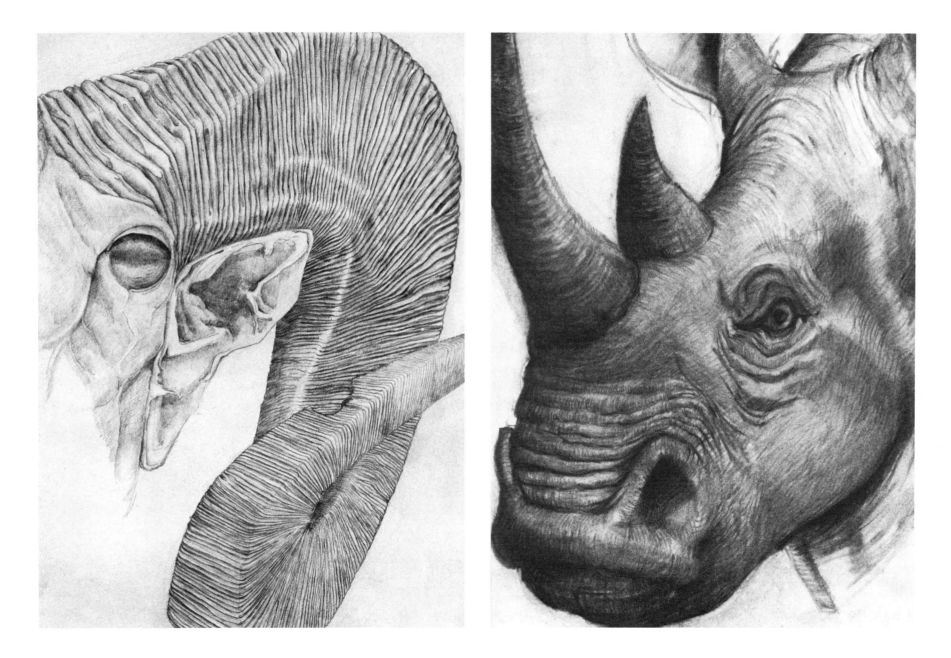

Figure 69. Paula McLay Maynes.
Photo: David Aschkenas.

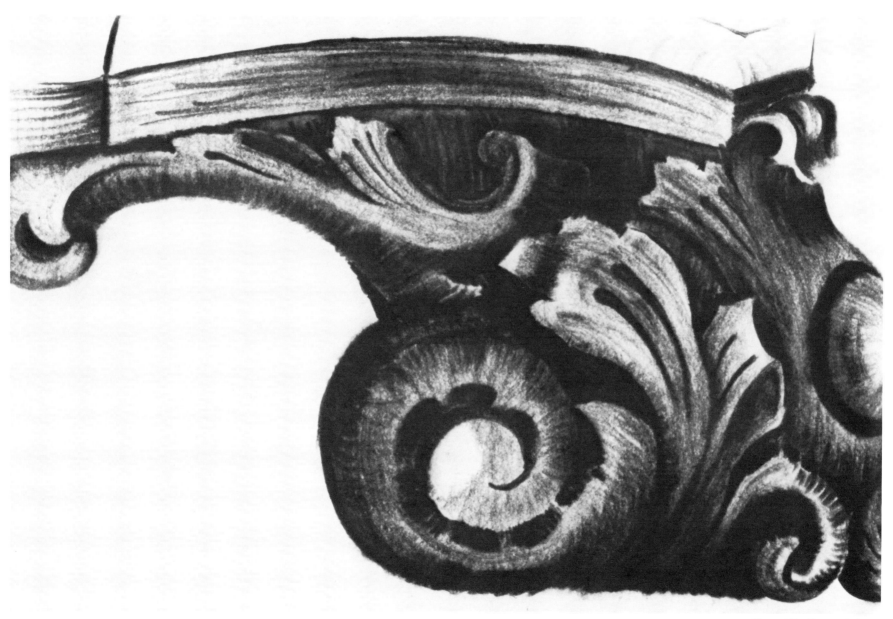

Figure 70. George Athens.

PICTORIAL DEPTH CUES

Having gained understanding of texture, Gibson's precondition for visual perception, we move now to inquire as to how we are able to perceive space on the basis of combined textural gradients. With his guidance, we will consider the characteristic signatures of the information of the visual field, the *depth cues,* and their relation to drawing. The first of these is *upward position in the visual field.*

Upward position in the visual field *Response to the tendency of objects, seen against a ground surface, to be positioned higher in the visual field with greater distance.*

Upward position in the visual field is an optical derivative of *linear perspective* . It is conditioned on several characteristics of the visual field within our environment. Because of gravity and because we live on the earth's surface, most what we see in daily life tends to be located on or near the ground surface. Moreover, our upright posture dictates that most of what we see tends to be seen against that surface as a background as well. Thus chairs, tables, and the like usually appear located against the continuous background of the familiar floor on which they sit, and we are able, consequently, to represent basic spatial relationships merely by locating things higher (for farther) or lower (for nearer) in pictures we make.

Figure 71. *Ostriches.* The lower ostrich is nearer. The higher ostrich is farther.

In effect, drawings using *upward position in the visual field* reflect a mental map of the world that combines plan and elevational views into one expression. The elevational surfaces contribute visual profile and a sense of recognition; the plan surfaces contribute location and a sense of place. In the more complex uses of drawings by architects and designers, *upward position in the visual field* forms the basis of our spatial understanding of all paraline views (see chapter 4, axonometric, isometric, and oblique views, pp. 138–151).

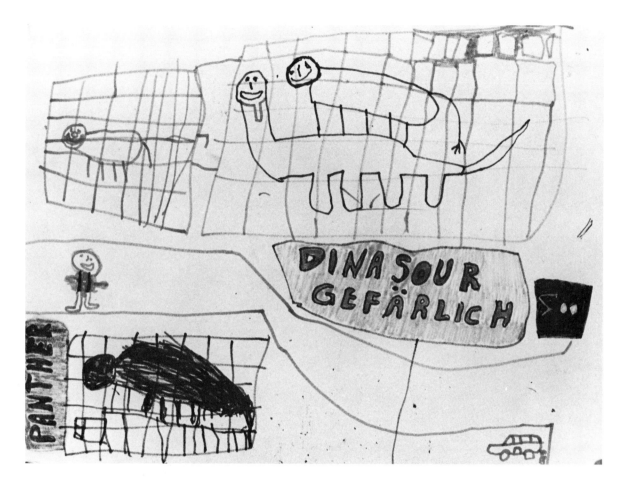

lated problems. The first is mnemonic;[9] they must recall the absent thing. The second is representational; they must record the absent thing so as not to forget it even as they reconstruct it. As the cue of choice in this process, *upward position in the visual field* is ideally suited to serve as a twin memory prod and note taker. Because it is neutral as to projected shape and size, things can be recalled and recorded in any orientation, with true shape and scale retained as desired. Because it readily accommodates sectional views, relevant interior parts can be recorded as recalled; because it does not fix the point of view, recall can proceed independently of locational constraints.

Given the ease with which it represents position and appearance, it is not surprising that *upward position in the visual field* should be the first depth cue commonly used by children. It is used as early as age five, but this use goes beyond the question of its accessibility and rests on its support for the functions of childhood drawing.

Figure 72. *At the Zoo.* The lower bird is nearer. The higher dinosaur is further. Drawing: Laura Cooper (age 6).

Young children rarely, if ever, draw from life. Rather, they draw things at some point after experiencing them as they are able to reconstruct them.[8] Drawing something from memory presents two simultaneous and re-

[8] At that age, drawing from life would seem needlessly redundant. Given the understanding of drawing as making that is developed in the next chapter, the sheer lunacy of drawing something already present should be apparent. Why should they draw it when it's already there?

[9] Having to do with the process of memory.

PICTORIAL DEPTH CUES

Overlap *Response to the tendency of near objects to overlap far objects.*

According to Gibson, readings of overlapping edges arise in abrupt shifts of textural gradient, from the gradient of the material in front to that of the material behind. Of the pictorial cues, *overlap* is the most definitive. It establishes what is in front of what. Though not foolproof,[10] *overlap* has a unique veracity among the pictorial cues that owes to its relationship with *motion parallax*.[11] Things overlap each other at their edges. Edges are likewise those sites within the visual field where, under conditions of movement by the observer, the most visual agitation would be expected to occur. It is there that the greatest relative ocular movement or shear (near object appearing to move rapidly across a far object moving slowly) is found, or *would be found if only we could move*.

With this last phrase, I seek to express the sense that *overlap* captures the pertinent information of one instant of *motion parallax*: On this potent basis, flats in theater stage sets

[10] Given a stationary viewer, readings of overlap function either according to prior knowledge of the shapes in the field or, lacking the former, according to the law of simplicity so valued by gestalt psychologists. Both of these processes can be easily tricked.

[11] Motion parallax is a response to apparent relative motions of objects at various distances from the observer when the observer is moving.

60

and paper cutouts in children's pop-up books produce convincing spatial representations, though as individual pieces they may be crude and without depth. Likewise, on this basis simple line drawings are able to achieve a potent sense of visual life.

Figure 73. (opposite page) *Two Birds.* The near bird overlaps the far bird.

Figure 74. *Interior at the Schultz'.* Simple line drawings represent the pertinent information of one instant of motion parallax. Drawing: Rebecca Schultz.

PICTORIAL DEPTH CUES

Shade and shadow *Three dimensional modeling of objects in light, shade, and shadow.*

Though differences between the two are obvious, *shade and shadow* function on the same information base as *disparity vision.*[12] Both rely on the view from two distinct positions in space. In the case of *disparity vision,* the second eye provides that other view; in the case of *shade and shadow*, the sun. By indicating, from the point of view of the sun (or some other source of light), what would be overlapped, i.e., shadow, and what would be out of sight though not overlapped, i.e., shade, *shade and shadow* provide what amounts to three-dimensional stereoscopic information.

Shade and shadow are different in terms of the information they provide. In general, shade provides information only about surface, while shadow provides information about both surface and location:

1) *Shade can indicate shape:* A gradual modeling from light to dark within a shaded surface indicates a rounded surface. An abrupt transition from light to dark indicates a faceted surface.

[12] Disparity Vision: the primary cue that operates on the basis of the disparity between the views of the two eyes. It was well demonstrated by the nineteenth-century invention, the stereoscope.

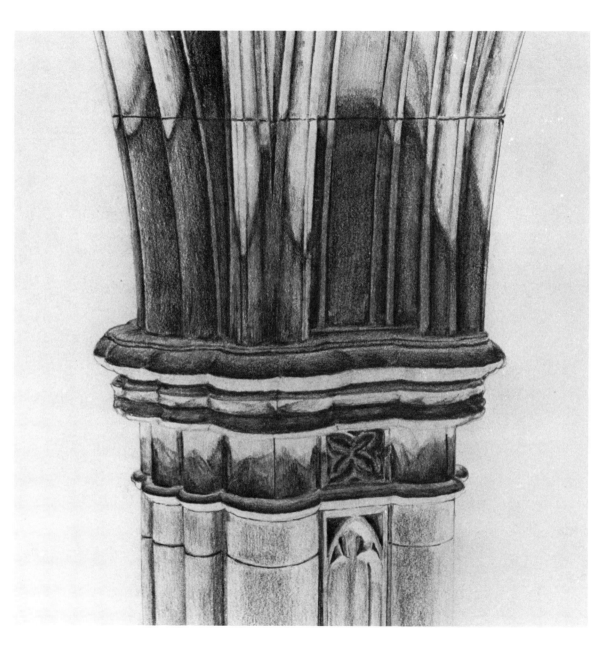

2) *Shade can indicate surface orientation:* Under some conditions, the darkness of shading indicates the degree to which a surface is turned away from a light source

3) *Shade and shadow can indicate surface quality and relief:* A surface casting shade and shadow upon itself indicates roughness; a surface casting no shade and shadow upon itself indicates smoothness. A mountainous landscape casts shade and shadow into its valleys, but a plain cannot.

4) *Shadow can indicate shape:* The edge of a shadow forms a contour line on the object receiving the shadow. The form of that contour line gives information about the shape of both the object casting the shadow and the object receiving the shadow. A serrated knife casts a serrated shadow, even on a flat surface. A round object receives a rounded shadow, even from a straight-edged object.

5) *Shadow can indicate the relative position of objects:* An object that touches the shadow it casts also touches the surface receiving the shadow, but an object that does not touch the shadow that it casts also does not touch the surface receiving the shadow. A man leaping off the ground disengages himself from his shadow.

Figure 75. (opposite page) *Gothic Leaves.* Shade and shadow can indicate surface shape and relief.

Figure 76. *Column Capital.* Shade and shadow can indicate surface shape. Drawing: Harvey Butts.

PICTORIAL DEPTH CUES

Size perspective *The apparent reduction in size of objects of known size with greater distance from the observer.*

Size perspective is optically related to *linear perspective*. It reflects the reduction of the projected sizes of objects and material textures with greater distance from the observer, much as *linear perspective* reflects the convergence of parallel lines to common vanishing points.

In the picture at right, which has a layered definition of depth similar to the drawing on the opposite page, the larger auto and larger house are nearer, the medium-size house is farther, and the small house is farthest.

Figure 77. *Lower Greenfield.* Depths are defined by the projected sizes of objects whose real size is known.

Size perspective appears occasionally in the drawings of young children as a way of achieving a sense of great depth. In the drawing at left, abrupt shifts in size yield a layered sense of depth. The nearest layer consists of the wagons, horses, and riders. The second layer consists of the castle. A third layer consists of the distant houses.

Figure 78. *Houses and Wagons.* Depth as a consequence of three distinct projected sizes of objects.
Drawing: Sarah Cooper (age 6).

PICTORIAL DEPTH CUES

Aerial perspective *Response to the effect of air on the color and visual acuity of objects at various distances from the observer.*

Of the pictorial cues, aerial perspective is the most painterly. Its information varies as a condition of the context, rather than as an absolute condition of the object itself. It arises in the fact that the light reflected from distant objects must pass through more atmosphere to reach the observer than the light reflected from nearer objects. Two effects are produced:

1) *Distant objects appear bluer.* The materials of the intervening atmosphere (oxygen, water, and dust) tend to more effectively obscure the more distant object, supplanting it, in effect, with their own reflected light, the blue color of our own familiar sky. This effect is evident in the common practice in landscape painting of adding greater amounts of blue with greater distance.

2) *Distant objects appear less distinct.* In obscuring the more distant object, the intervening atmosphere is also intercepting the light reflected from that object. The information from the more distant object is thus

less complete. Bright surfaces appear grayer. Dark surfaces appear grayer. Sharp outline and detail are less pronounced.

Possibly owing to its subtlety, aerial perspective is one of the last cues to emerge in drawings. It is at the root of such tricks as line weight shifts (heavier lines denoting nearer and lighter lines denoting farther) that are commonly used in the orthographic and axonometric conventions of architects and designers.

Figure 79. (opposite page) *Steel Mill.* The nearer parts of the mill are more distinct. The distant hills are less distinct.

Figure 80. *Aerial Perspective.* George Caleb Bingham, *Fur Traders Descending the Missouri,* oil on canvas, The Metropolitan Museum of Art, Morris K. Jesup Fund, 1933. (33.61)

PICTORIAL DEPTH CUES

Linear perspective *The apparent convergence of parallel lines to common vanishing points with increasing distance from the observer.*

In Gibson's terms, linear perspective is a reflection of the *visual field* rather than the *visual world.* It approximates how we see (the retinal image) rather than what we see (the objects in the world before us). The image at right shows tracks converging, one big train and one little train, and trapezoidal passenger cars, but we perceive tracks extending into the distance, a near train and a far train, and rectangular passenger cars.

The potency of such perspective views arises in their ability to capture a visual moment in a way that is specific to one individual, in one position in space, and in one moment in time—a powerful immediacy. I confess that the train at right still seems to leap out of the page at me much as it did when I first saw this same view as a child of six. As a convention of freehand drawing, linear perspective is the last pictorial cue acquired, and it is rare to see evidence of its use before age seven. Among those who do continue to draw habitually into adolescence, it is usually reasonably well understood by age twelve, although its tricks are sometimes difficult for even these more experienced drawers.

Figure 81. *Spirit of America.* Grif Teller. Perspective captures the visual moment.

Years of teaching architectural students indicate that difficulties in mastering linear perspective owe to the aforementioned discrepancy between sensation and perception (i.e., how we see, the retinal image, versus what we see, the objects before us). This conflict may be understood as a conflict between appearance and knowledge. Despite its appearance from the direction of the view of the photograph to the left, we still know that an elephant has one trunk, two eyes, two ears, four legs, and one tail; despite our knowledge of the elephant shown in the drawing to the left, an elephant may still appear to have one trunk, one eye, one and one half ears, three and one half legs, and no tail. This conflict, which is fundamental to representations generally, is made all the more difficult for novices of perspective to resolve because of the uses and conventions of early childhood drawing which tend to give greater emphasis to knowledge over appearance and often remain as vestiges at a later age.[13] One such vestige is the recurrent dominance of *upward position in the visual field* as a prime pictorial cue. As in the two views of the space to the left, this emerges as a tendency to rotate the floor surface upward toward the viewer in perspectives of deep spaces.

Figure 82. *Two Elephants*. The knowledge of an elephant versus the appearance of an elephant.

Figure 83. *Two Views of the Same Hall*. Vestiges of childhood conventions are evident in the up-tilted floor. Photo: Raymond Mall

---

[13] See *upward position in the visual field*, pp. 64-65.

FREEHAND PERSPECTIVE

My own introduction to linear perspective came as a result of a subscription to a magazine about trains I received as a child of six. This magazine was filled with photographs similar to the calender painting by Grif Teller in Figure 81. To my six-year-old sensibilities, these photographs seemed as alive as the very moment of a train's arrival. So impressive were these views that I tried to make drawings like them, and the frustration of these attempts is something I remember to this day. On one occasion, I remember tearing at my shirt lapel with such fury that the buttons flew off my shirt and landed one by one around the room.

This short tale points to the difficulties involved in learning to draw in linear perspective. As has been already indicated, these difficulties can be traced to confusion about differences between the *visual world* (the actual size and shape of the things we are drawing) and the *visual field* (the projected size and shape of those same things). Overcoming them requires great concentration upon the shape of the visual field and on the underlying geometric construction. Two tips: Begin with a spatial armature; proceed methodically with foreshortening.[14]

1. Begin with a spatial armature

Always begin with a freehand drawing of the underlying geometry of the space. In the case of a one-point perspective, this underlying

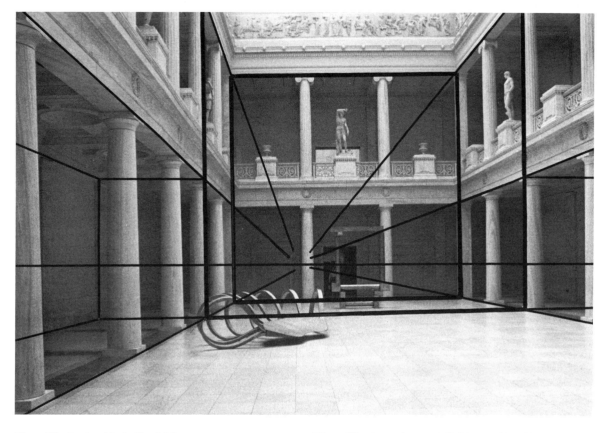

Figure 84. *Begin with the Spatial Armature.*

Figure 85. *(opposite page) Halving and Doubling Intervals.*

geometry is generated off what serves as the end-wall condition of the view in tandem with the central vanishing point of the view. (See *Exercise 3, One-Point View,* pp. 76-77, for further details.) In the case of a two-point perspective, it is generated off what serves as the corner of the view in tandem with the two vanishing points of the view. (See *Exercise 4, Two-Point View,* pp. 78-79.) In both cases

you should quickly establish a host of converging guidelines to serve as an armature over which the view can proceed. These lines should be generated with two contradictory thoughts in mind: they should be sufficiently controlled to give structure and precision to the view, but they should be sufficiently loose to retain the sense that your drawing is a freehand and active record.

2. Foreshorten by halving or doubling

Find a repetitive elemental order in the scene before you. This order may be present already as a material texture or structural framework, or you may impose it. Based on the diagrams at right, foreshortening can proceed in two ways from these elements.

---

[14] *Foreshortening:* Apparent reduction in the size of surface elements with greater distance from observer.

Halving intervals (Fig. 86. left): Guess a large interval with an even number of parts (four column bays). With diagonals, divide this interval into two halves. Using the same method continuously applied, subdivide these intervals into smaller units. *Doubling intervals (Fig. 86. right):* Guess a small interval (one column bay). Find the mid-point of an opposite side. Extend a diagonal from one corner of the interval through that mid-point, thus doubling the original interval.

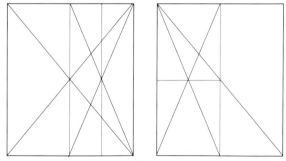

Figure 86. *Geometry of Halving and Doubling.*

3. Measure projected angles and distances

Throughout the process of generating a perspective, you have to measure projected angles and lengths. Before beginning, remember that the projected angles and lengths you see before you are likely to differ from the actual angles and lengths of the object you are drawing. What is in fact 90° probably does not project as 90° in the perspective view; what is in fact a square probably does

Figure 87. Measuring Projected Angles and Lengths.

not project as a square. Whether measuring projected angles or lengths, you should begin by imagining that you are viewing the scene before you through a large sheet of glass that has been placed perpendicular to your line of sight at a comfortable distance from you. In both cases, you should conceive of making the measurements on that glass window. This window is called the picture plane.

Measuring projected angles (above left): Use your pencil as a protractor of sorts. Place it over the optical angle you wish to measure, measure it (usually it makes sense to think of it as measured off the vertical or horizontal), and then transfer that angle to your drawing. *Measuring projected lengths (above right):* Use your pencil as a ruler. Superimpose it over the distance in question and measure its length along the pencil. Then transfer that projected length to your drawing.

discussing some of Nicholaides's exercises on mass and volume. It was pointed out that these exercises gave a sense of immediacy to the act of drawing, a sense that the thing being drawn was physically present on the page, and out of that an understanding of *drawing as an act of making* was developed. Likewise, this concept ought to be introduced into the discussion of perspective at an early point. For reasons that were raised in the introduction to chapter 1, architects and designers must maintain a wary suspicion of any approach to drawing that is built solely on sensibilities that are purely visual. Because their activities are ultimately rooted in the act of building, their drawing must proceed on a basis that models that act. If perspective is to make any contribution beyond final presentation, its most trivial usage, then it must likewise embody the act of constructing, and from the ground up. It is through a process that begins with the geometric armature that this sensibility enters the process.

4. Develop the view over the armature [15]

Figure 88. *Spatial armature.*   Drawing: Li Hang Wang.

Having built the armature from the underlying geometry of the scene before you, develop the perspective right over that armature. The perspective should be conceived as hung over that armature, much as a coat is hung on the armature of a coat hanger or a curtain wall is hung on the structural frame of a building. Do not be concerned that the armature is still visible through the drawing.

Because it gives information as to the process through which the drawing was generated and because it serves to clarify the underlying geometrical relationships of the space shown in the view, the armature should remain visible.

Underlying the idea of the geometric armature is an idea that was introduced briefly in

[15] I want to acknowledge the contributions of Professor Bruce Lindsey and, indirectly through him, Professor Philip Grausman of Yale University for my understanding of the geometric armature. A presentation of Grausman's drawing course can be found in: Mark Rylander, "The Importance of Perspective Drawing in the Design Process," in *Crit XV*, edited by Laura Todd, Washington, DC.: American Institute of Architectural Students, Inc., 1985.

FREEHAND PERSPECTIVE
Exercise 1
Pure Surface Texture in Perspective [16]

The study of perspective all too easily becomes mired in analysis to the point that the act of seeing becomes lifeless, and in the process we lose all that Nicholaides urged us to build. Therefore, before beginning the study of perspective, it is best to revisit (in a modified form schooled by our exposure to Gibson) the first exercises in his sequence on contour. These exercises should be repeated regularly throughout the sequence of perspective exercises that follow.

Begin by choosing an architectural scene that is characterized by legible textural gradient at multiple scales (e.g., bricks, windows, and houses) and a significant depth of field. Then look at some point within the scene before you and, at the same time, imagine that your pen is actually touching that point within the textural array. Let your eyes slowly move along the textural gradients before you, and, in one continuous line and *without looking at the page,* let your pen follow the movement of your eyes as they follow the textural gradient in the scene before you. As you draw, believe that your pen is actually touching the surfaces of the scene.

Materials: Ebony pencil or lithographic crayon.

---

[16] Adapted from "Pure Contour," in Kimon Nicholaides, *The Natural Way to Draw,* pp. 9-10.

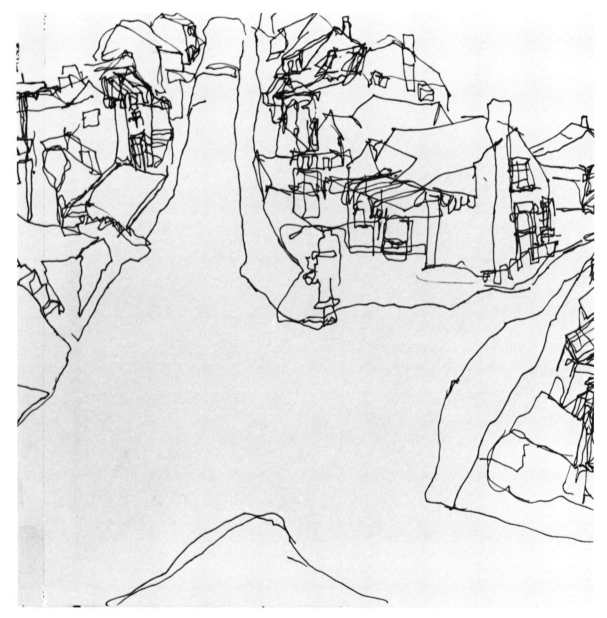

Exercise 2
Modified Surface Texture in Perspective [17]

Draw the textural array as you did in the previous exercise, but glance occasionally at your page as you draw. While you should avoid turning this exercise into an exercise dominated by analytical construction, do try to gain a sense of the feel of convergence while you do this exercise. In a way that is related to gestural drawings, try to get your hand to mimic convergence.

Materials: Ebony pencil or lithographic crayon.

Figure 89. (opposite page) Rebecca Schultz.
Figure 90. Rebecca Schultz.

---

[17] Adapted from "Pure Contour," in Kimon Nicholaides, *The Natural Way to Draw,* pp. 9-10.

FREEHAND PERSPECTIVE
Exercise 3
One-Point View

Go to a long, rectangular interior space that is characterized by repeated intervals of architectural elements, such as doors, windows, or structural bays, as might be found in the nave of a church or an industrial warehouse.

Draw the geometry of the space first. Begin with a freehand drawing of the geometry of the end wall. It should include information such as overall proportion, centerlines of columns, and heights of major elements. It should remain abstract, and the lines should have the character of guidelines. They should be carefully drawn in a light line weight but should also remain sufficiently loose to retain the spirit of a freehand exercise.

Locate a point on the end wall opposite your own position. Because you are looking parallel to both side walls of the space, this point will serve as the central vanishing point for the view. Draw a horizontal line through this point. This line is the horizon line, which represents the horizon as we would normally understand that term in daily life. It also represents the height of the viewer, your height, in the view. Draw a set of light lines radiating out from the central vanishing point. Within this set, emphasize those lines that are pertinent to the geometry of the space.

Indicate intervals of depth in the view. They might be based on structural intervals (e.g.,

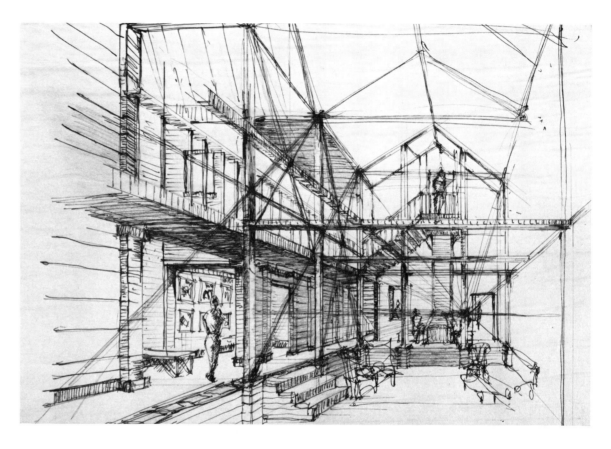

Figure 91. *One-Point Perspective Using Doubling and Halving Intervals to Foreshorten Depth.* Catherine Carr.

columns) or surface intervals (e.g., openings), or some regular interval that you have simply imposed on the space. Then use one of the two methods outlined earlier, doubling intervals or halving intervals of foreshortening, to extend the intervals of depth of the armature out toward you.

Now you can draw the perspective representation right over the geometric armature. As described on the previous page, the perspective should be conceived as hung on that armature, much as a coat is hung on the armature of a coat hanger.

Materials: Felt-tipped pen, bond paper.

An alternative method to foreshorten depth is the *magic method*. This method is described in greater detail in chapter 4 (see pp. 172-173), but it is readily adapted to freehand use. It uses regular floor intervals to extend the drawing forward into the space and requires less guesswork than the method just explained. Begin by drawing the end wall in the manner just described on the previous page (with a horizon line and lines converging at the central vanishing point). Then extend the horizon line out to the left or right of the body of the drawing. Measure out along that line (to the left or right) an estimate of your distance from the end wall. This point is the vanishing point for a spatial diagonal on the floor. On the same side as this point and along a line extending out from the base of the drawing of the end wall, estimate (at scale) the increments of depth (e.g., struc-

Figure 92. *One-Point Perspective Using the Magic Method to Foreshorten Depth.* Li Hang Wang.

tural grid or floor tiles) you wish to foreshorten. This line will serve as a distance ruler. Measure foreshortened increments of depth by projecting lines from the vanishing point for the diagonal, through increments along the distance ruler to points along the base of the side wall.

FREEHAND PERSPECTIVE
Exercise 4
Two-Point View

Go to an interior space that is characterized by a strong diagonal direction of view and by repeated intervals of architectural elements such as doors, windows, and structural bays.

Draw the geometry of the space first. At an appropriate size, represent a major corner in the space with a light vertical line. At a height appropriate to the height of your point of view relative to that corner, draw the horizon line through this vertical. At points to the left and right of the corner, locate vanishing points for the two spatial axes of the space. In locating them, note the orientation of your direction of sight relative to the space. There are three basic conditions: If you are looking into the corner at an angle approximately 45° to either side, the two vanishing points will be approximately equidistant to either side of the corner (Fig. 95). If you are looking more nearly parallel to the wall to your left, the vanishing point on the left will be further from the corner and the vanishing point on the right will be closer to the corner (Fig. 96). If you are looking more nearly parallel to the wall to your right, the vanishing point on the left will be closer to the corner, and the vanishing point on the right will be further from the corner (Fig. 97).

Next draw sets of light lines radiating out from the two vanishing points. Within these sets, emphasize those lines that are pertinent

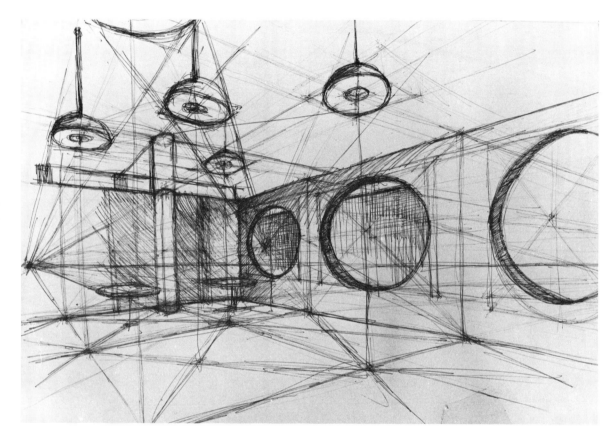

Figure 93. *Two-Point Perspective Using Doubling and Halving Intervals to Foreshorten Depth.* Li Hang Wang

to the geometry of the space as it extends out toward you. Then indicate intervals of depth in the view. They might be based on structural intervals (e.g., columns) or surface intervals (e.g., doors, windows, or floor tiles), or they might be based on a regular interval that you have simply imposed upon the space.

Use doubling intervals of foreshortening or halving intervals of foreshortening to extend the intervals of depth of the armature out along the two side walls. As in the one-point views, now proceed to draw the perspective representation right over the geometric armature.

Materials: Ebony pencil or felt-tipped pen, bond paper.

Though it steps beyond what can be immediately seen (indeed, it even steps outside the space that is shown), an instructive two-point view is a bird's eye view looking down into a space. I have found these are actually somewhat easier than two-point interiors for novices to do, perhaps because they make the building appear somewhat more like an object they can easily visualize (i.e., they are no longer inside the thing they are drawing). The sense of the armature and the sense of constructing the building on the page are more accessible as well.

Figure 94. *Two-Point Bird's Eye View.* Nicholas Tyson.

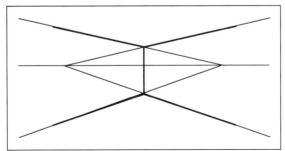

Figure 95. *Two-Point Equiangular View.*

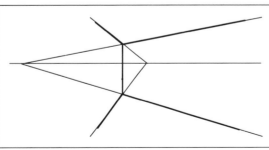

Figure 96. *Two-Point View More Parallel to Left Wall.*

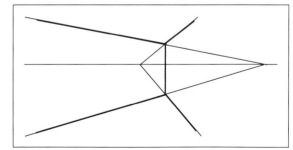

Figure 97. *Two-Point View More Parallel to Right Wall.*

79

FREEHAND PERSPECTIVE
Exercise 5
One-Point View of Stairs

Find an interesting stairway that is characterized by articulate spatial intervals such as
structural bays or landings. Position yourself
so that you are looking up the run of stairs.
Using the methods outlined in *Exercise 3,
One-Point View,* draw the stairway as a one-
point view.

In constructing the diagonal path of the stair,
consider that path as a question of rise and
run, that is, as a question of projected height
versus projected depth. At some point in this
process, you should start to note the position
of the vanishing point for the diagonal of the
stair, the vanishing point that governs such
diagonal elements as the banister and the
stringer. You can, in effect, extract it from
the view by extending these elements to their
natural point of intersection. Because you
are drawing a stair moving up and away from
you, that point is located above the central
vanishing point. If you were drawing a stair
moving down and away from you, the vanishing point for the stair would be located
below the central vanishing. In fact, the
example at right extracts that vanishing point
as well.

Materials: Ebony pencil, bond paper.

Figure 98. Sung H. Kim.

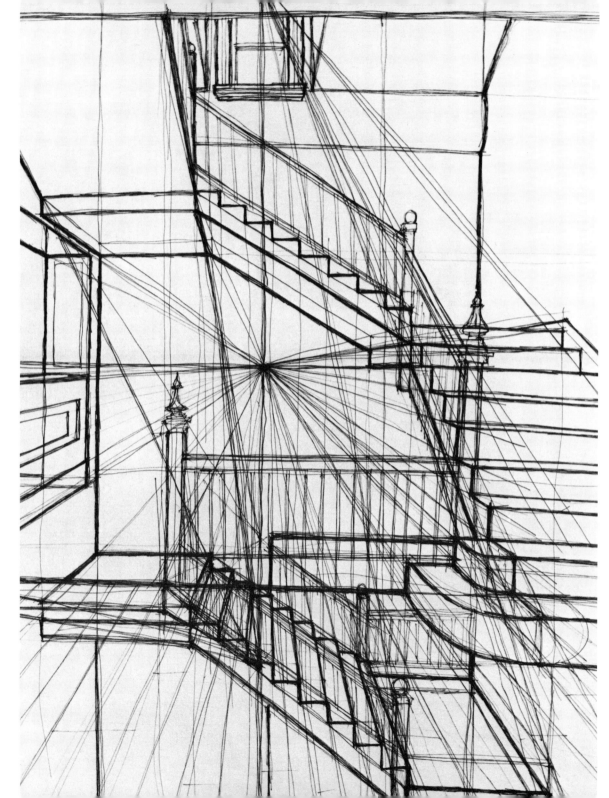

Exercise 6
Two-Point View of Stairs

Find an interesting stair that turns at 90° at its landings. As in previous exercises, the stairway should be characterized by articulate spatial intervals such as structural bays and landings. Position yourself so that you are looking up the run of stairs. Using the methods outlined in *Exercise 4, Two-Point View,* draw the stairway as a two-point view.

In constructing the diagonal path of the stair, consider that path as a question of rise and run, that is, as a question of projected height versus projected depth. At some point in this process, you should start to note the position of the vanishing points for the diagonals of the two or three runs of stair. They will be the vanishing points that will govern such diagonal elements as the banister and the stringer. You can, in effect, extract these from the view. In the case of a stair moving up and away from you, it will be located above the appropriate vanishing point for that spatial axis. In the case of a stair moving down and away from you, it will be located below the appropriate vanishing point for that spatial axis.

Materials: Ebony pencil, bond paper.

Figure 99. *Two-point view of stairs.*

FREEHAND PERSPECTIVE
Exercise 7
One- or Two-Point View up the Street

The pair of exercises on these two pages
builds on the understanding of locating vanishing points of diagonal elements that
originated in the previous stair exercise. Find
an interesting uphill street scene in a mixed
residential-commercial district. Choose a
scene with lots of elements that have under-
sides, such as porch roofs and shop awnings.

Using methods outlined in previous exercises,
draw the view up the street. As you draw, pay
careful attention to vanishing points of diagonal elements: the street itself, automobiles,
sidewalks, and telephone and electrical wires.

Materials: Ebony pencil, bond paper.

Figure 100. *Corner of Mission and Barry.* Two-point view
up the street.

82

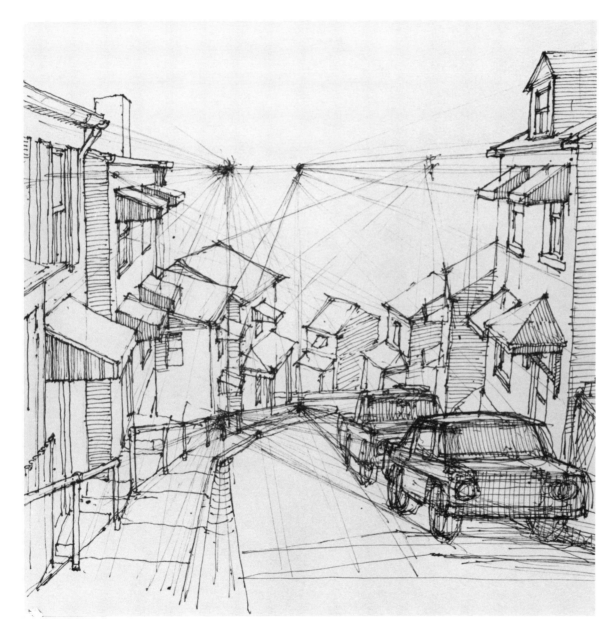

Exercise 8
One- or Two-Point View down the Street

Find an interesting downhill street scene in a mixed residential or commercial district. Choose a scene with lots of elements that have topsides, such as porch roofs and shop awnings.

Using methods outlined in previous exercises, draw the view down the street. As you draw, pay careful attention to vanishing points of diagonal elements: the street itself, automobiles, sidewalks, and telephone and electrical wires.

Materials: Ebony pencil, bond paper.

Figure 101. *Corner of Mission and Barry.* Two-point view down the street.

FREEHAND PERSPECTIVE
Exercise 9
Imposing Perspective on Rounded Forms

Until now most of the things we have drawn have lent themselves easily to perspective. They have been rectangular and composed, with few exceptions, of straight line elements. Before moving to natural forms (the focus of the next exercises), we will consider objects that are composed of curved elements.

Begin by choosing a hand tool or machine tool that has significant curved elements, cylinders, or parts of cylinders, or cones. Then draw the tool through a process of imposing a rectangular order on that object. Where it has circles, generate them by inscribing them in squares which you have constructed first in perspective. Where it has irregular shapes, generate them first as regular shapes in perspective and then measure their deviation from those regular shapes accordingly. As you proceed, it is important that you actively consider all that you draw as an instance of an artificially imposed x, y, z coordinate system.

Materials: Ebony pencil or felt-tipped pen, bond paper.

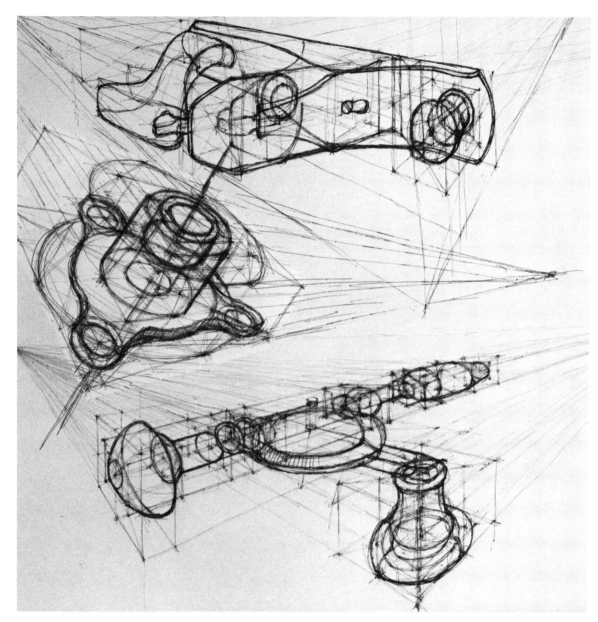

Figure 102. Chris Neighbor.

84

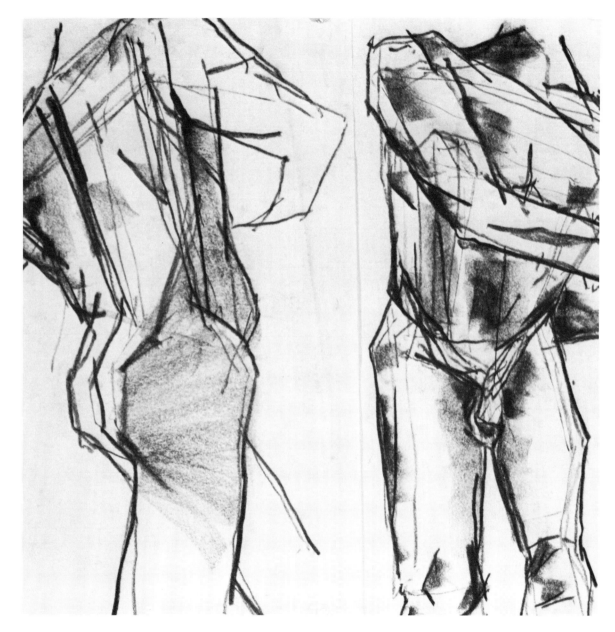

Exercise 10
Imposing Perspective on the Figure

Before moving out into the landscape, where forms are less accepting of the imposition of perspective, we will impose it first on something closer at hand: the human figure.

The model will take a pose in which elements of the pose are foreshortened. With line as the basic element (you may use shade and shadow as a means to clarify facets and sectional cuts) and in a manner similar to your work in perspective in the previous exercises, draw the pose or elements of the pose as an instance of perspective. As you draw, try to articulate the figure through a process of imposing a perspectival order on the model; that is, think of the *natural* form of the human body as an instance of an *artificial* x, y, z coordinate system and consider the drawing as progressing from that underlying geometry to physical form.

Materials: Ebony pencil or felt-tipped pen, bond paper.

Figure 103. Lisa Aufman.

FREEHAND PERSPECTIVE
Exercise 11
Imposing Perspective on the Urban Land-scape

Find an interesting uphill or downhill scene in which buildings have been inserted into a natural setting. Look for a scene in which elements such as roadways, automobiles, stairways, and the buildings themselves serve to articulate the slope and orientation of the landscape. As you draw, try to represent the scene as something that is made articulate by human intervention, that is, by the imposition of the x, y, z coordinate system in the form of the buildings and roadways in the scene.

Materials: Ebony pencil or felt-tipped pen, bond paper.

Figure 104. *Corner of Mission and Barry.* Imposing perspective on the urban landscape.

Find an interesting uphill or downhill rural scene. Look for a scene with *few* elements such as roadways or buildings that might serve to articulate the slope and orientation of the landscape. As you draw, try to articulate the landscape (trees, rock formations, and ground forms) through a process of imposing a perspectival order on that landscape and on these natural elements. Despite the geomorphic and biomorphic character of all the forms in the landscape, you are to think of this *natural landscape* as an instance of an *artificial* x, y, z coordinate system.

Materials: Ebony pencil or felt-tipped pen, bond paper.

Figure 105. *Bryce Canyon.* Imposing perspective on the rural landscape.

FREEHAND PERSPECTIVE
Exercise 13
Extending beyond the Limitations of
Perspective's Single View [18]

As has been already discussed, perspective
documents the momentary view looking in
only one direction from only one position.
Under certain circumstances, even when we
might not wish to change locations, this
limitation can seem severe. One such circumstance would be a scene that invites both
looking to the left and looking to the right,
for example, the joining of two roads at an
acute angle at an intersection. Another would
be a scene that invites both looking up and
looking down as would be the case at a landing
of a stair or at a highway switchback in a
hilly landscape.

Seek out such a condition. Represent it as a
binocular drawing, that is, a drawing having
one station point (position of the viewer) and
more than one direction of view. Whether
you use line only or whether you use the more
tonal approach of the examples from my own
work shown to the right, try to treat each view
as distinct even as you try to join the two
views into one unified composition.

---

[18] This assignment builds on an assignment given by Professor Kent Bloomer, now of Yale University, that I encountered as a student studying architecture at CMU (then
Carnegie Tech) in Pittsburgh. A more detailed discussion of
that assignment appears in the next chapter.

Figure 106. *South Side Bend.* Douglas Cooper, 1989,
carbon pencil on paper, 56" x 80" (private collection)
Photo: David Aschkenas.
This scene is the hill overlooking Pittsburgh's Southside at
the bend between Barry and Holt streets. The bend in the
road, the sweep of the view, and the inclination of the views
are typical of the Pittsburgh landscape. In executing a view
of this sort, attend to each of the two views separately before
trying to reconcile them. Distortions are to be expected in
the areas between the views; worrying about them prematurely only causes problems.

Figure 107. (opposite page) *Two Gates.* Douglas Cooper,
1985, carbon pencil on paper, 80" x 112" Photo: David
Aschkenas.
This scene is opposite the south entry to the main piazza in
Siena. Observe that each portal has its own vanishing point,
and that each is at a different height. That of the left portal
is higher and contributes the sense of looking down; that of
the right is lower and contributes the sense of looking up.
For those who attach meanings to such things, the road on
the left leads down to the city cemetery and that on the right
up to the banking district.

FREEHAND PERSPECTIVE
Exercise 14
Extending beyond the Limitations of Perspective's Single Point of View [19]

As with its single direction of view, perspective's restriction to one point of view (position of the viewer in space) can, on occasion, also seem limiting. Even in generating what might be called faithful perspectives, sliding the point of view slightly is sometimes quite desirable and reasonable in order to compensate for the limitations of the view from any one position. However, this assignment goes well beyond such reasonable limits as these to the point that the viewer's moving becomes the most important issue in the drawing.

Find some interesting space that offers support for viewing from several positions. The space could be as large as a hall, as is true of the drawing immediately to the right, or as small as a room. What is important is that you should be inspired by the space to want to view it from a number of positions. Then try to draw the space as an accumulation of the several views from the several positions. As part of your process, you should actively enforce this multipositional sense by actually moving to different positions as you draw. As you do so, try to treat each view as distinct even as you try to join the several views into one unified composition.

---

[19] Like the previous one, this assignment also builds on the assignment from Kent Bloomer. See chapter 3.

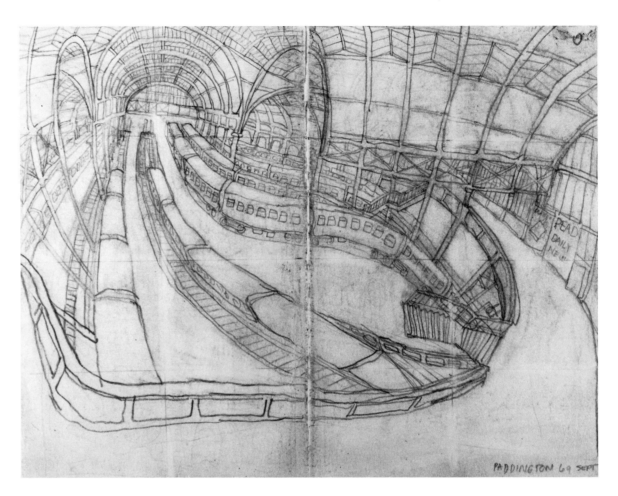

Figure 108. *Paddington Station.* Douglas Cooper, 1969, 8" x 10" (from the author's sketch book) Photo: David Aschkenas. This view was drawn from two positions along an overpass within Paddington Station in London. The first looks to the right and was positioned to the right of the train at the center. The other looks along the length of the shed and was positioned to the left of that same train. You may notice that the train seems to twist as a consequence.

Figure 109. (opposite page) *Bar Leading Upstairs.* Douglas Cooper, 1985, carbon pencil on paper, 80" x 112" (private collection) Photo: David Aschkenas. This drawing, generated originally in a Victorian pub in London, records the view from five positions: two sitting in each of the couches in the foreground, two above the two couches in the foreground, and one above the lantern at right.

LIGHT AND DARK

Having learned to think of drawing as a process of making and having learned to build objects from the ground up, we are now in a position to proceed with the question of appearance and with that most ephemeral of qualities, light. Before we begin this subject, two principles must be stated. In the spirit of the tactile foundation we began with Nicholaides, we must retain a sense of the spatial armature that has formed the basis of our work in perspective. In the interest of focused observation and clarity of composition, we must retain a strong sense of *overlap*, the depth cue introduced earlier in this chapter.

1. Retain the spatial armature, and a sense of gesture and contour

The danger always lurks in the background that attention to light will lessen the constructed basis that has been central to our approach so far. Light is material's opposite, and, as perceived, it is a superficial phenomenon, literally on the surface. Therefore, even as we clothe the things we draw in light, we must continue to bear in mind the material

Figure 110. Christine Malecki. Figure 111. Neil Kittredge. The spatial armature should precede drawing light and dark.

core beneath. As represented by the pair of drawings above, early drawings in light do well to proceed from preparatory underdrawing that represents the spatial armature.

Contrast is also a matter of conception in the sense that we must apprehend light in a way that sharpens distinctions. In both views at left, the spectrum of values has been both simplified (treated in high contrast with minor distinctions leveled) and greatly expanded (from darkest dark to lightest light) so as to serve pictorial intentions advantageously.

2. Use contrasting value as a device to reinforce contour and overlap

Figures 112 and 113 Hans Hillmann. Illustrations from *Fliegenpapier* (Fly paper)[20]

Contrast is a matter of both composition and conception. It is a matter of composition in the sense that we must arrange the scene, through point of view or positioning of objects, such that overlapping edges are made apparent by dark areas juxtapositioned with light areas.   In the two views above, the before and during of a bar room brawl in an

illustrated version of a gangster story, the arrangement of light and dark is carefully choreographed to maximum spatial effect. In the scene at left, light overlaps dark and vice versa to affix a stiffly layered sense of spatial tension. In the brawl at right, the same device is used to effect a richly layered and confused image of chaos.

[20] *Fliegenpapier* is the German translation of Dashiell Hammett's *Fly Paper,* illustrated by Hans Hillmann (Frankfurt am Main: Zweitausendeins, 1982) pp. 27, 34.

As we proceed in our study of light, the importance of cross-contour to our reading of form will be underscored. We will find that light offers useful information about form largely because it, in effect, draws cross-contours on the forms that it shades and shadows. The following three exercises direct attention to these surface contours, the first through a process of simplification enforced by the use of simple media.

LIGHT AND DARK
Exercise 1
Imposing Two Values on the Figure

Describe the surface of the model as either dark (black ink) or light (blank page). As you draw, try to interpret the dark space in such a way that it serves both to suggest the form of the light space by implication and to suggest the overall form of the model by drawing significant contours on its surface. With respect to this issue, pay close attention to three factors: 1) the point of view that you choose (pick a direction that has articulate shades and shadows), 2) where you choose to draw the line between light and dark, and 3) the way the view is framed in the page.

Materials: India ink, calligraphy brush, bond paper

Figure 114. Katherine Ruffin.

Exercise 2
Imposing Four Values on the Figure

By using four values, the following exercise greatly increases the subtlety of range available. Nonetheless, the need for considered observation of where to draw the line among the intervals is no less important. Indeed, it is only made somewhat more difficult.

Describe the surface of the model as either darker (black ink), dark (umber), light (ocher), or lighter (blank page). As you draw, try to interpret the shapes of the areas of dark and light in such a way that they serve to suggest the form of the figure by drawing articulate contours on its surface. With respect to this issue, pay close attention to three factors: 1) the point of view that you choose (pick a direction that has articulate shades and shadows), 2) where you choose to draw the line between light and dark, and 3) the way the view is framed in the page.

Materials: Calligraphy brush, black watercolor, umber watercolor, ocher watercolor, watercolor paper (can be of low quality).

Figure 115. Riitta Vepsalainen.

LIGHT AND DARK
Exercise 3
Chiaroscuro: Working from the Middle Out

On account of the media used, the two pre-vious exercises have proceeded from starting points of absolute brightness, the state of the untouched paper at the start of the exercise. Likewise, the analysis of light within each exercise proceeded from an extreme end of the available spectrum. As a consequence of the background paper it uses, the following exercise introduces a new starting point: the middle of the light spectrum.

Working with white and black Prismacolor on gray charcoal paper, describe the full range from dark to light on the surface of an object of your choice. Choose the study object and its lighting carefully for its capacity to sup-port this exercise. It must have a variety of articulate shapes of dark and light, and it must have a sufficient range from dark to light. As in previous exercises, try to inter-pret the shapes of the areas of dark and light to suggest the form of the figure. With respect to this issue, pay close attention to three factors: 1) the point of view that you choose (pick a direction that has articulate shades and shadows), 2) where you choose to draw the line between dark and light, and 3) the way the view is framed in the page.

Materials: Black Prismacolor, white Prismacolor, gray charcoal paper 20" x 24".

Figure 116. Yahwee You.

96

Exercise 4
Value and Hue: Unlimited Pallet

In considering the issue of light and dark, the previous exercises have avoided the question of hue altogether. Necessarily so, for the question of color lies beyond the scope of this book. However, color is an important issue for the question of light and dark if for no other reason than for demonstration of the extent to which value (ie., light versus dark) is independent of hue (coloration in the sense of blue, red, and yellow). The analysis within the following exercise is built upon that independence.

Find an interesting color photograph of a rural scene. Then with color scraps torn from magazines and glued onto a sheet of illustration board, try to replicate the appearance of that original photograph. As you proceed, try to separate the issue of value from the issue of hue.

Materials: Color magazine scraps, paste, illustration board 15" x 20", at least.

Figure 117. Yvette Kovats.

LIGHT AND DARK
Project
A Catalog of Appearances

Using primarily watercolor, develop a catalog of drawings investigating the reciprocal
interactions of:

1) *Window:* size, shape, depth, material, and
orientation.

2) *Room:* size, shape, width, depth, height,
material, and orientation.

3) *Light:* time of day, season, weather, and
orientation.

4) *Exterior conditions:* ground surface,
planting, and neighboring structures and
conditions.

Figure 118. Marybeth Barrett.
Figure 119. Jean Geiger.
Figure 120. (opposite page) Robin Kohles.
Figure 121. (opposite page) Kenneth Heinz.

3
Beyond
Appearance

Formal Implications of
Why We Draw

BEYOND THE LIMITATIONS OF APPEARANCE

Thus far we have addressed the question of learning to see in parallel to learning to draw. Initially, at Nicholaides's urging, we considered drawing as an activity that must follow upon intense physical involvement with objects drawn. Then, in a more analytic approach built on Gibson, we used his understanding of the order of the visual field as a basis. However, neither direction has raised the question of why we draw. We have provided a foundation for drawing technique that is firm, but we have yet to inquire about its purposes. This inquiry is the focus of what follows. It will begin at the beginning, with drawings of early childhood, and in the process it will develop our understanding of drawing as an act of making, an idea that has only been touched upon so far.

Childhood Arguments

I was in the second grade when the question of the purpose of drawing first arose, though initially in the guise of a question of technique. I got into an argument with my best friend, Toby McCarthy, about linear perspective. Both of us had drawn pictures of military airplanes (this would have been during the Korean War), and what ensued between us was no small fight in itself. My airplane was drawn in proper second-grade perspective, from the side with wings foreshortened and the far wing partly obscured by the fuselage.

His, which appeared hopelessly primitive in my eyes, was also drawn from the side, but the wings were drawn as if from above and all four engines were fully in view. Of course, the great debate, in which ours was just one small skirmish, was the argument over appearance and reality. Should drawings intend to represent appearances or should drawings intend to represent reality?

Technique or Intention

The argument might first appear to be more about technique than intention. This certainly would have been my view at the time, for I believed our intentions to be the same. We were both drawing airplanes, and, with a self-righteousness that only a six-year-old can muster, I believed mine to be better drawn. But what are the intentions of drawing at this age? What might these intentions imply for the intentions and forms of drawings generally?

Let us consider two children, John and Sally,[1] who are drawing pictures of cabins. They soon fall into an argument, but here the argument does not turn on technique. Something else is at stake. The argument begins with a dispute about attributes. John's cabin has a basement and Sally's does not.

---

[1] One of a set of drawing sessions recorded at McEwan Open School, Pittsburgh, March-May 1980. The names of participants have been changed for the sake of privacy. The text is abridged.

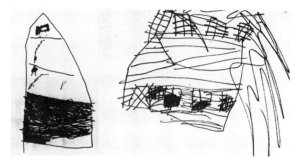

Figure 122. John, age 5 (left), Sally, age 5 (right).

John: *Anyway, you don't know at all about cabins.*

Sally: *I know about cabins, and I know how to make cabins.*

John: *I made a cabin already (with) a window (and) all these floors.*
What do you think a big cabin is?

Sally: *Cabins don't have any floors. They only have one downstairs.*

John: *Nuh-uh!*

Sally: *Yes, I've been in a cabin. I'm making a different cabin. It's better than that.*

John: *That's not how you make a log cabin.*

Sally: *It is. Look for yourself. There's a log cabin. Look for yourself, if you want.*

John: *Anyway, I know what log cabins are. They're made out of logs.*

Sally, daughter of an architect, now takes on the question of materials.

Sally: *Big cabins aren't always made out of logs. They're also made out of plastic logs.*

John: *Nuh-uh! They're made out of wood.*
Sally: *This is not really a kind of log cabin. It's a kind of plastic log cabin.*

After returning to basements for a while, a game of "can you top this" with respect to chimneys follows:

Sally: *They have a lot of fireplaces. We have a lot of fireplaces . . . and lots of chimneys.*
John: *We've got . . . we've got three chimneys.*
Sally: *We've got more than that.*
Child: *How about a million chimneys?*
Sally: *I don't got that.*
Child: *How about a hundred chimneys?*
Sally: *I don't got that.*
John: *What do you got?*
Sally: *I said there's one, two, three. Three chimneys.*

John begins darkening in his basement.

John: *I'm making all this dirt. This is a basement and with black dirt. That's what they have under basements for real.*
Sally: *I know it's not dark in basements. They have light.*
John: *No, our basement has spiderwebs. Yikes! Oh, yikes!*

John suddenly leaps to his feet and runs down the hall in mock fright at the spiderwebs. When he returns, Sally, by now convinced that cabins can have basements and more

importantly spiders, reaches into John's basement, grabs an imaginary spider, and chases John back down the hall, all the while holding the spider at his back.

It is plain that these children are engaged in a debate and that something important is at stake. Whether intentionally or not, the children are using drawing to support a speculative and freewheeling debate about the concept *cabin*. At issue is the question of the parts and relationships necessary to acknowledge an instance of the *idea* of cabin. Along the way a number of proposals, many of them contradictory, are put forth. These proposals address questions of major parts: Basements, *yes or no?* Material, *wood or plastic?* Attributes? *Lots of chimneys won the day*, and attributes of parts? *Spiders seemed accepted as a useful if scary attribute of basements.*

For its impact on the form of these drawings, the following observation is key. The activity of drawing is both imaginary and real: imaginary in the sense that things drawn and discussed are not present, but real in the sense that things that are virtually present are acted upon as if physically present. When Sally pulls a spiderweb from John's basement, that spiderweb is treated as real. John treats it as such by acting as if he were afraid.

It would seem that the words *drawing* and *picture* in the sense that we usually use them do not apply to this argument. With these words, we usually mean (I believe mistak-

enly) a kind of secondhand and diminished version of the thing in the picture, hardly a description adequate for Sally and John. On the contrary, these children seem to be *making* cabins. In fact, they even use the word *make* throughout to characterize what they are doing, and making these cabins appears to empower them to deal with the idea of cabins.

A Sculptor's Drawing Assignment

Some years after my original argument with Toby McCarthy, the question of intention in drawing recurred. I was a student in a drawing class in architecture school when Kent Bloomer, now of Yale, gave the class an assignment well outside my abilities in perspective. Bloomer asked that in one drawing we show everything inside and everything outside the classroom. He intended, of course, to require using drawing in a new and hence instructive way, but there was clearly more to the assignment than this common pedagogical prod. The rich content of the assignment had much to do with Bloomer's background, and in its own way that background would serve to reinstate for me the same use of drawing that we observed in John and Sally's drawings of cabins.

Bloomer is a sculptor. In fact, he had never taught drawing before this course, and he brought a certain skepticism about drawing to the class. Although I have never questioned him on this point, I would attribute his skepticism to a natural distrust of the tricks and limitations of working in two dimensions by one accustomed to working in the real space of three. While it would be unfair to say that Bloomer questioned the worth of drawing per se, he certainly did question the use of perspective. His criticism indicated as much, and he referred us regularly to the pictorial space of medieval and proto-Renaissance painters such as Lorenzetti and Simone Martini for models to pursue. For our purposes, the key feature of their work was their use of orthographic conventions to show several locations simultaneously. In any event, the bias against perspective was already implicit in the assignment. In that the assignment could not be solved by drawing the view from one position, perspective was, in effect, out of consideration from the start. Like the sculptor's sense of a piece as a sequence of views, our drawings would have to represent seeing as a kinetic sense. Many of the examples in Bloomer's criticism referred to sculpture. The thought occurred to me that he somehow wanted our drawings to be more like sculpture. Why?

The Question behind the Assignment

Bloomer's assignment had reopened the old discussion that had been at the crux of my argument with Toby McCarthy: *reality versus appearance*. This question is central to the history of Western art, and nothing so dominates the discussion as Plato's passage in the *Republic* that condemns the work of the painter as lowlier even than that of the furniture maker. Plato considered working with concepts to be the highest of activities.

To the extent that they depended upon the senses, he distrusted all other activities. He particularly distrusted painting. Even the furniture maker, Plato allowed, in making a bed, does transform the idea of a bed into a particular instance of bed; at least in this sense the furniture maker must work with a concept. By contrast, the painter, in transforming the appearance of a particular bed into a picture, need not bother with a concept at all but only with an instance: the bed before him. His work, Plato argued, is twice removed from reality: first in dealing with an instance of a concept and second in dealing with the appearance of that instance.[2]

It could be argued that Plato was really condemning all representational art, sculpture included, in that sculptors, after all, do work with appearances. But Plato reserved his condemnation for painting. Given Bloomer's background as a sculptor and the character of his assignment, the question arises, Why painting and not also sculpture?

I suspect that an answer may be found in comparing the work of the sculptor to that of the painter in a manner parallel to Plato's earlier comparison. The sculptor, like the furniture maker, also makes objects. What he makes is matched to the entirety of a reference (360°) rather than a single view. To argue the point as Plato might, whereas the sculptor is twice removed from concepts, first in dealing with an instance and second in dealing with the appearance of that instance, the painter is really thrice removed from concepts, first in

dealing with an instance, second in dealing with the appearance of an instance, and third in dealing with one aspect of that appearance.

To read Plato's words in the *Republic*, we might even get the impression that something about painting is sinful. Once he characterizes painters as deceivers of children.[3] At the very least, Plato dismisses painting as trivial entertainment. Now, while I know Bloomer well enough to state that he would not condemn something solely for its sinfulness, and I know that he views drawing as a serious activity, I do suspect that something of a reformist was at work. With his assignment, he may have been trying to upgrade drawing to the level of sculpting where it would become more an act of *making* an object and less an act of *imitating an appearance* of an object. What are the implications of making drawings that are more like things and less like appearances?

An Assist from E. H. Gombrich

Among the many who write about art and its history, few have written with such consistent clarity as E. H. Gombrich. Gombrich has written much about the fundamental nature of art, and for our purposes in considering drawing as making, what stands out is his formulation of a representation as a substitute. Briefly stated, this model presents the process of representation as one of matching a substitute to a reference. In this process, making precedes matching. For example, in making a snowman, we begin by first piling snowballs on top of one another, and only then do we begin to match the pile to whatever degree of likeness is desired.[4]

What is so useful in this model is that it allows for any degree of likeness to occur without inconsistency with its formulation of the process. At one end of a spectrum of likeness, we might stack three snowballs, call it a snowman, and simply leave it at that. Then again, we might spend the afternoon carving a highly detailed figure and insist on giving it a coat. Greater or lesser degrees of likeness are accounted for in the greater or lesser degrees of specificity of the schemata (the attributes and parts in relation necessary for recognition of the reference) that we bring to the process. Effectively, then, Gombrich's model releases pictorial representation from an intention of making appearances, an intention Plato (and I at age six) may have unfairly given it in the first place. Likewise, it gives it a new intention, that of making and matching a substitute (a thing in its own right) to a reference, an intention more compatible with the sculptural analogy Bloomer had been suggesting. Gombrich goes on to discuss the formal implications of substitutes generally.

In his brilliant essay, "Meditations on a Hobby Horse," Gombrich outlines a test for any substitute, its use in substitution. Although this test has much to do with schemata, in this essay Gombrich particularly emphasizes the act of using as the ultimate test. For him the test of a hobbyhorse is whether it can be used as a horse, that is, whether it is rideable. Gombrich distinguishes this question from the question of its appearance, whether it is a broomstick found in a closet and called a horse or whether it is an heirloom with a carved head and reins.[5]

What then must a drawing do as a substitute? *What its reference does*, must be Gombrich's answer. It must be able to take the place of the thing in the picture, yet in a sense it must also do more. Much as a hobbyhorse affords the possibility of riding for those otherwise too small to ride (something a real horse could not), a drawing must empower us over its reference. A drawing of a cabin must enable five-year-old children to argue and speculate about the nature of cabins, activities less possible in the presence of a real cabin and its unyielding authority as an instance. Likewise, a drawing of an airplane must allow the construction of an airplane for those Toby McCarthys of the world who are too young (or too poor) to buy the parts, and a drawing of a building must enable an architect to build, tear down, and rebuild (with graphite and paper) the interim solutions that a client could not afford to build if they were executed in real bricks and mortar.

What of the intention of my rival view of the airplane? While my work in the interim has shared Toby's intention, if I could turn the clock back, I would intervene to observe that he was using drawings to make airplanes and that I was using drawings to make airplanes appear to fly. While I might now envy his drawing and believe its intention worthier, I might still acknowledge that, for a six-year-old, making an airplane seem to fly out of the page is a form of empowerment too. Are these two intentions, which I might state as *making it appear* and *making it be,* irrevocably at odds? I think not. To borrow phrases associated with Jerzy Kosinski and Gertrude Stein, the challenge is to create *the sense of being there* and at the same time *a there, there.*

Chapter 3

The drawings that follow provide examples for the preceding essay. Many are by children; others are my own late submissions to Bloomer's assignment. Whatever their origin, in the spirit of this volume as text, all drawings are presented as submissions to retro-assignments. While they do not constitute a pedagogy, they do sum up the essence of Bloomer's assignment and do intend to assist students beyond replication of appearances.

[2] Plato, "The Republic," in the *Dialogues of Plato*, translated into English by B. Jowett (New York: Random House, 1937), book X, pp. 852-879.

[3] Plato, *Dialogues of Plato*, p. 855.

[4] E. H. Gombrich, *Art and Illusion*, 2d ed., Bollingen Series XXXV, No. 5 (Princeton: Princeton University Press, 1961), Chapter 3, pp. 93-115.

[5] E. H. Gombrich, "Meditations on a Hobby Horse or the Roots of Artistic Form," in *Aspects of Form*, ed. Lancelot Law Whyte (Bloomington: Indiana University Press, 1966) pp. 206-228.

DRAWING AS RECALLING

Draw to Remember a Place

In classical antiquity, courses on memory expansion used architectural subjects as elements of pedagogy.[6] In a time when paper did not exist to record such simple things as shopping lists, to say nothing of three-hour orations, an ability to remember things and to remember them in order was no small matter. In these courses, students were instructed to seek out a building (ones with clear plan sequences were preferred) to use as memory vessels. They were to commit a path through their building to memory. Then, when they would wish to memorize a speech, they were instructed to assign the various parts of that speech appropriately to the various parts of their building. In general, a parallel was sought between the hierarchical structure of the building and that of the speech. Whole sections might be assigned to major halls, paragraphs to niches, sentences to figures, and so on. In reciting the speech, the orator would need only to imagine walking through the building to recall the words in order. Though operating in reverse order, this assignment reestablishes this ancient union between memory and architectural subjects.

The two reconstructive drawings shown here arose from different conditions. One was reconstructed from long-term memory, the other from short-term. The former (shown above) was drawn by a student of mine and shows a nunnery that was across the street from the house where she grew up. It was

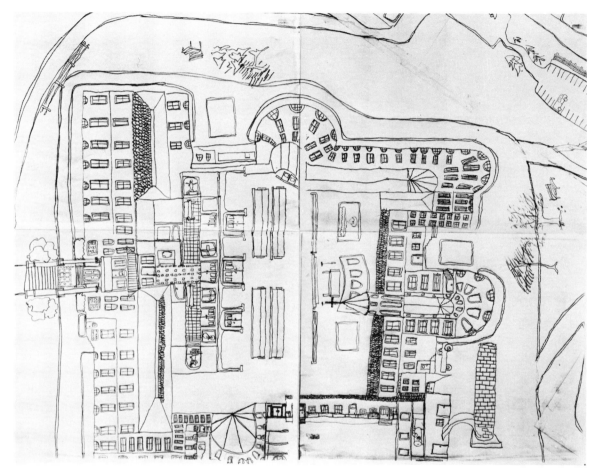

drawn over a period of several weeks. Characteristic of such exercises of memory, it is not specific to any one point of view. The latter (shown on the opposite page) I drew in cooperation with my wife, Meg. It arose out of dire circumstances. On our last day of visiting Rome, we had arrived late at Trajan's Market. The guard was not only tired but drunk as well and wanted to go home. Bribes were able to secure only a visit of one-half hour maximum, after which, the guard yelled after us as we entered, the gates would be locked. There would be no time to draw. So Meg and I agreed that she would go one way and I another. After rejoining, I did the above drawing from our shared accounts.

Figure 123. (opposite) *Sisters of St. Francis.* Joan Lasky Saba.
Figure 124. *Trajan's Market.* Meg and Douglas Cooper, 1969,
8" x 10" (from author's sketchbook). Photo: David Aschkenas.

Figure 125. Sarah Cooper (age 6). Facsimile of drawing from period described below.

Tuesday, 22 September: We are eating breakfast in a hurry because we have overslept. Sarah (age 7) is eating waffles with maple syrup. I am crouched under the dining room table tying her shoes while she eats. Abruptly Sarah starts talking about amusement park rides. (During the last week she has shown me a series of drawings of roller coasters like the above. She knows my queasiness about these rides and has been using her drawings to find out which rides I might like.) As she talks, I observe from the movement of her elbow that she is drawing one of these rides in the maple syrup covering her plate.

For whom was this ephemeral ride in maple syrup intended? Surely it was not for me: my head was beneath the table. More likely it was for her. Reenacting riding must have served to make talking about roller coasters easier.

Sadly, one of the most interesting drawings I could present for this assignment on reconstruction no longer exists. It vanished even as it was being made and is shown here only as a facsimile. This drawing, which was of a roller coaster ride, was interesting not only as a device of recall but also for its implications for the origins of gestures (of the sort made in giving street directions to someone unfamiliar with a neighborhood) and their relationship to drawing.[7] It is also interesting as an embodiment of pure movement.

[6] This method is called the method of loci. It is discussed in Francis A. Yates, *The Art of Memory* (Chicago: University of Chicago Press, 1966) pp 1-50.

[7] This drawing implies that such gestures are vestigial drawings, drawings recreated not for the one receiving the directions, for whose understanding they are likely unimportant, but as a memory prod of sorts for the person giving the directions.

107

DRAWING AS MAKING

Draw and Make Whole Things

Before we can act on a thing as if it *were* present on the page, we have to believe that it *is* entirely there. It must be wholly present before us. If the elephant has four legs, two ears, two eyes, two tusks, one trunk, and one tail, then these parts must all be present for the thing itself to be present. Likewise, as in the drawing at right, if a tree has roots, then they must also be shown, whether they would be hidden by the ground or visible.

This drawing was done as a part of the normal second grade daily routine by my eldest daughter, Laura, when she was a student at the Waldorf School, a Rudolf Steiner School, in Frankfurt am Main, Germany.[8] Rudolf Steiner pedagogy is insistent on proceeding from whole things to partial things. In arithmetic, learning whole numbers precedes learning fractions. In addition, the sum is always written to precede the addends: $4 = 2 + 2$, rather than $2 + 2 = 4$. Among the sciences, physics, which studies mechanical interactions of whole things, is introduced in the sixth grade, well before chemistry, which studies compounds and is not taught until the seventh grade.

Within the field of painting and drawing, the idea that whole things should be considered before partial things extends beyond just the nameable parts. It pervades their use of color and their understanding of the very materiality of the drawing itself. Under the direction

Figure 126. Laura Cooper (age 8) second grade class book, Waldorf School, Frankfurt am Main, Germany.

of her teacher (he opened the exercise with a story to this effect), the earth was considered as made from three elements: sky (blue), light (yellow), and fire (red), and was drawn as a mixture of these colors. When the tree was drawn, it was shown as pulling these three elements up the trunk into its branches, where finally only two elements remained and the tree achieved its most skylike expression in the combined effect of light and sky: green.

We have encountered this idea earlier in a different form. The reader will remember that, in chapter 1, Nicholaides's exercises on mass reflected a similar sequence. Before proceeding to manipulate mass, students were first asked to do the massing exercise, whose purpose was to establish the materiality of the

Figure 127.
Room in Niederwald.
Joerk Haberman.

charcoal they would subsequently manipulate on the page. Whatever their scientific correctness (and this was certainly not their point), we note in both exercises an attribution of *real* material properties to the media of a drawing. We can *make* things with them because they are materially present.

In that it reflects a more purely visual sense of inclusion, the above line drawing of a room is a sublimation[9] of the material processes just described. However, in a manner similar to the first drawing's retention of the roots of the tree and in a manner similar to the characterization of the drawing of the elephant, this drawing is equally insistent on the inclusion of all requisite parts. While it is certainly a record of what was seen, it seems even more compelled by a requirement to record all that is there, whether seen or unseen. The word inventory is the best description; we are left convinced that all parts are present and accounted for.

---

[8] Rudolf Steiner developed his approach to education in the early part of this century after much study of Goethe, whose writings on Botany he had edited, and against the background of the formative years of gestalt psychology. Steiner's insistence on a holistic approach is consistent with both.

[9] Elevated from a more primitive state.

DRAWING AS USE

Drawing as the Act of Moving

The drawing at right of a slide in a playground by my youngest daughter, Sarah, is interesting for its orderly process as well as for its support of movement. With a kind of real-world logic, making the slide precedes using it. When she does it, in this case climbing and sliding on it, that use is recorded with the marks she makes; note the dots where she climbed the ladder. On the day Sarah made this drawing, I was in the room and recorded what was said on a concealed tape recorder. She talked throughout the process, sometimes to me but more generally to herself. Her words are instructive as a reflection of her thinking.

Figure 128. *Playground.* Sarah Cooper (age 6). A drawing that enacts an act of moving. Photo: David Aschkenas.

I'll make a swing set.
I'll make some children in it (and) in the playground.
Two children are sharing this swing.
There's a big swing set with this curling sliding board.
(drawing the curling lines across the page)
You go back up again . . . and you slide.
(moving down the slide with her marker)
And you slide. And you go up.
You go down . . . down, down, and down.
(She calls suddenly to me.)
Daddy, how do you like this slide?
I'll show you how you go on this slide.
You go up these stairs
(She climbs the stair with her marker. Note the dots.)
And then you go like this,
Go like that, and then you curl.
(Her voice fades and she is no longer talking to me.)

Then . . . that way. Hey, Woopsa!
Get all squished up there.
(reaching the bottom of the slide)
Then you go up again. You go up here . . .
Go like that and then . . . you're out.
This is all the boots. (drawing at the base of the slide)
The children come out and fall off.
Then you need to walk in deep water.

110

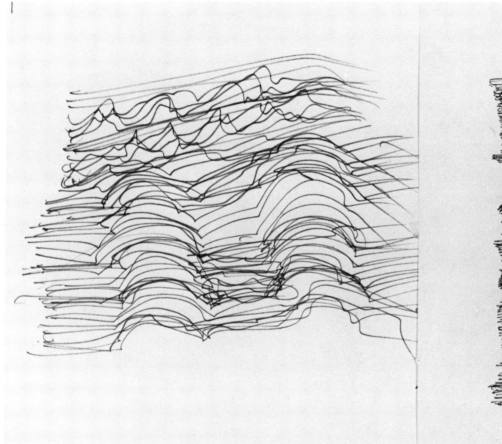

The pair of drawings above are sublimations of the more primitive relative to their left. In the example of the slide, the movement the drawing records is real in the sense that the marker represents a person actually climbing and sliding on the sliding board. On the other hand, the two above, though no less convincing as records of movement, are one step removed from that degree of immediacy. They record how the marker *would* move *if it were* touching the surface of the building. In this conditional but compelling sense of the real they get at the heart of what Nicholaides was after. In effect, they show the next step: how to transfer the *real-time* immediacy of the slide into a drawing that records vision.

Figure 129. *Iroquois Building* (one drawn quickly the other slowly). Douglas Derr. Drawings that record vision as an act of movement.

111

DRAWING AS RECALL, MAKING, AND USE

Do a Drawing that Shows Everything Inside and Everything Outside

In short form, this title is the original assignment from Kent Bloomer, and it involves elements of the three previous retro-assignments. From my own work, the works shown here and on the overleaf come closest to fulfilling that assignment as it was originally given. For the purposes of going beyond appearances, which is to say, for the purposes of going beyond optics, the most important attribute of that original assignment was its requirement that we show more than one place. This bifurcation of focus had the effect of causing the visual field to close in on itself, for either one or the other or both of the two places. That closing (which is evident in both of the drawings at right) effectively precluded any approach that would seek to report only the *visual field*. Our drawings were forced to address the *visual world* (as distinct from the visual field) and, as a consequence, took on the task of reporting visual journeys.

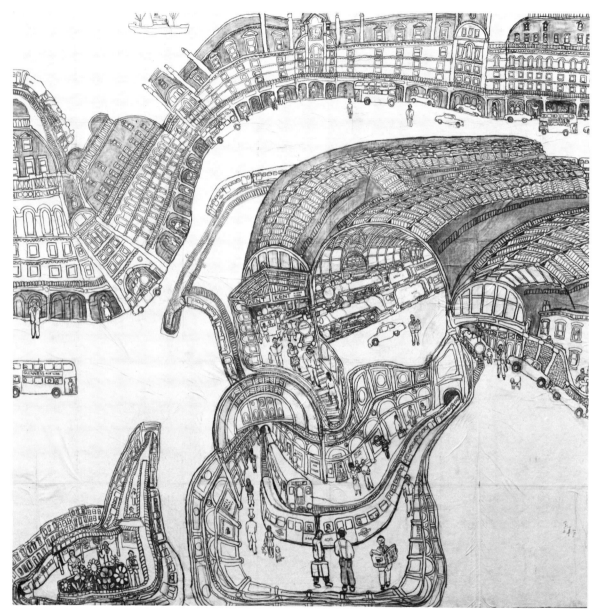

Figure 130. *From Paddington to Victoria.* Douglas Cooper, vine charcoal on bond, 1970, 72"x 96" (Collection Carnegie Museum of Pittsburgh).

Figure 131 (opposite page) *S. Maria delle Piave, Arezzo.* Douglas Cooper, 1971, 8" x 10" (from author's sketchbook). Photo: David Aschkenas.

112

Figures 132, 133, and 134. *Polish Hill*.
Douglas Cooper, 1989, charcoal on paper, 56" x 112"
(Collection Carnegie Museum of Pittsburgh).
Photos: David Aschkenas.

4
Conventions of Construction

A Guide to the Projective
Conventions of Architects and
Designers

DRAWINGS AND DESIGN PROCESS

Good Questions

Good architects and designers are said to ask the right questions at the right time, but just how and when do their questions arise? As a background to this section on architectural drawing conventions, I propose that their questions are generated in part by the act of representing itself and that, through adjustments of scale and levels of imprecision that are natural to a process of representing in miniature, drawing plays an active role in controlling the flow of questions, answers, and tests throughout the design process.

A Painter's Advice

I still remember the advice from the instructor of a portrait class that I took years ago. He urged us to never allow any one feature or part to become significantly more complete than another. Instead, we should carefully maintain a consistent level of completeness (or incompleteness) across the whole portrait. The process he proposed was one of repeated iterations, each of which would be more refined than its predecessor and each of which would resolve the entire face. To do otherwise, he warned, would be to risk irreparable distortion to complex relationships between any single part and the rest of the face. Anyone who has ever watched the slightest premature brushstroke on an eye turn a smile into a leer can attest to the soundness of his advice.

Painting a portrait is certainly no simple task. In effect, the painter juggles an infinite number of variables and tests, each of which changes dynamically throughout the process. In this characteristic, painting a portrait is not unlike designing a building. Perhaps a measure of my wise painting instructor's advice might be useful in considering the design representations of architects and designers as well.

Models of Design

Fundamentally, my instructor advised a recursive top-down strategy of decision making. Each successive iteration or cycle through the process first resolved relationships between major parts, then resolved relationships within each part, and finally readjusted relationships between the major parts once again. We might, for example, have begun with an underpainting of umber wash to establish relationships of value exclusive of questions of hue; then we might have proceeded with overpainting in color; finally we might have readjusted the relative lightness and darkness of those colors to reestablish the relationships of value of the original umber wash underpainting. The underlying purpose of such a strategy would have been to reduce the number of relationships we novice painters would have had to consider at any given time. At any point in the process, we would have been able to consider a set of issues in isolation—value, for example— without regard to hue. At the same time, owing to the recursive nature of the process, each partial

decision could have been resolved with respect to the whole face.

Note the part played by the physical act of painting in this procedure. In our example, the act of painting with a single hue had the effect of narrowing the range of issues to a manageable number. In fact, it could be said that the act of painting managed the process of painting by controlling its flow of questions, tests, and decisions. Could the same be said of the design representations of architects as well? Could their representations in a similar fashion also manage the process of design?

The Concept-Test Model[1]

Recently, the *concept-test* model of design has been advanced as an alternative to the troublesome *analysis-synthesis* model.[2] The most obvious advantage of this model is that it seems to parallel more closely the way architects actually work. For our purposes, its most striking characteristic is that its decision-making procedure is nearly the same as that advocated by my painting instructor for portrait painting. Like that procedure, the *concept-test* model is one of successive whole iterations. Briefly, design is understood as a recursive sequence of conjecturing and testing. The designer begins by proposing tentative solutions early in the process and progressively modifies them until they are acceptable. Testing occurs throughout the procedure and is viewed not only as a means to evaluate tentative proposals but also as a means to prod information gathering (at appropriate times) and to progressively refine criteria by which later proposals are to be judged.

Among other things, the *concept-test* model greatly emphasizes the importance of the act of representing a design. Inasmuch as the process this model sets forth is a reciprocating one (proposing leads to testing, which in turn leads to proposing), both processes propel each other. It would follow that the form in which a proposal is made could have a bearing on the nature of any test that might follow. In a manner similar to painting, it could determine what could be tested as well as what questions might be asked.

In light of the preceding, I am tempted to say that good architects make proposals in the right form to provoke the right questions at the right time. In this sense I am persuaded to entertain the possibility that design representations might also manage the process of design. For the purposes of argument, what follows will assume that to be the case so that the more interesting question of why they might do so can be addressed.

Substitutes[3]

In the sense that they take their place, all design drawings of buildings are substitutes for the buildings they represent. Magically, sometimes, in the moment that a model or a drawing is substituted for that unbuilt building, a new design has already been generated. Immediately the possibility arises (whether for better or for worse) that the reference will be changed in the process. This dynamic is fundamental to all representations.

In all substitutions, a certain measure of self-deception is involved. One thing is recognized as being of the class of another and used as if it were that other thing. To use a shoe to hammer a nail is for that one moment to have recognized a shoe as a hammer. The form required to trigger such recognition in error is a variable, and its specification is dependent upon need and availability. Where need is high and availability low, the range of recognizable substitutes is large. Oppositely, where need is low and availability high, the range of recognizable substitutes is small. Given a row of pictures falling off the wall and no hammer nearby, we might reach for a shoe. Given a long-avoided task and a full toolbox, we might even be selective as to which hammer we might use.

The potency of a substitute derives from the differences between itself and its reference. Such differences endow it with the capacity of enlarging the classification of whatever reference it replaces. For the moment at least, our friend using a shoe to hammer a nail has greatly enlarged the class of objects known as hammers by inventing a new one.[4] It is an invention whether others in less desperate circumstances think it is a good hammer or even recognize it as one. Insofar as it has been used as a hammer, it is a hammer.

Likewise, the architect who substitutes a drawing for an as yet unbuilt house has already invented a new house.

With such assertions, I wish only to establish that a representation is by definition a new design. Merely by taking the place of some reference, a substitute already sets up the prospect of change. However, the act of substituting alone cannot explain their ca-

---

[1] Stefani Ledewitz, "Models of Design in Studio Teaching." Unpublished paper presented at symposium on teaching, Pittsburgh, 1983. The concept-test model is credited to Donald Schon of MIT.

[2] This model of design, which received widespread attention in the late 1960s and early 1970s, presented design as a sequential process of information gathering, information analysis, program formulation, and finally product or building design.

[3] E. H. Gombrich, "Meditations on a Hobby Horse, or the Roots of Artistic Form," in *Aspects of Form*, ed. Lancelot Law Whyte, Bloomington: Indiana University Press, (1966) pp. 209-228.

[4] In some instances, a substitute may prove so successful at doing the job of its reference that it may eventually replace it in other contexts as well. Such is the way in which inventions gain currency. Like the instance of the hammer, they typically arise out of desperate circumstances: Years ago, ice cream sandwiches were popular items at kiosks along the boardwalk at Coney Island. One hot summer day, the demand for ice cream sandwiches was such that one salesman had nearly exhausted his supply of sugar wafers by midafternoon. He had much ice cream but few wafers. Not wanting to lose the afternoon sales, he decided to substitute one rolled wafer in the place of two flat wafers, thus creating the first ice cream cone. (Robert H. McKim, *Experiences in Visual Thinking,* Monterey: Brooks/Cole Co., 1972, p. 188.)

119

pacity to facilitate change in a design or how design representations might give the architect some measure of control over the process of design. Any explanation of the capacity of design representations to facilitate and control change must await a closer look at the physical characteristics of such representations, specifically, their size.

The Importance of Being Miniatures

Though it borders on stating the obvious, it must be recognized that most representations architects and designers use are miniatures. No doubt, time and budgetary considerations preclude the extensive use of prototypes and full-scale mock-ups and favor the use of more inexpensive miniature substitutes, but there are reasons beyond convenience and expense that explain their use.[5] Reduction in size is in itself significant.

In many cases, we overlook the fact that the size of a thing in large part determines the nature of that thing and, further, that any significant change in size entails fundamental formal changes. Several examples from zoology are instructive on this point. Suppose that a fly would become as large as a big mammal. Such increased size would require changes of proportion and the addition of new parts. With each tenfold increase of linear dimension, surface area would increase a hundredfold and volume a thousandfold. Like an elephant, our enlarged fly would need proportionally thicker legs to support its increased bulk. Where earlier its skin and

straight intestine would have provided adequate surface area for the absorption of oxygen and nutriment, our fly would now soon die of suffocation or malnutrition unless it could proportionally increase its surface area by evolving such additional parts as coiled intestines and multichambered lungs. What is true of animals is true of plants as well. Always we find that the smaller species are simpler, and the larger are more complicated. The simplest algae floating in stagnant water are simple round cells; larger plants, by contrast, require surface extensions, such as roots, branches, and leaves.[6]

Greatly increasing the size of a thing is necessarily an act of complication. Oppositely, and more importantly for our purposes, decreasing size is an act of simplification. Either fewer parts are needed or the complexity of those that still remain can be reduced. As simplifications, miniatures bring two capacities to the process of design that surround an apparent paradox in their nature. *With respect to their references, they are at once both less complete* (they have fewer parts, and they are more open ended, more suggestive, and more open to interpretation) *and more complete* (they are edited to a degree that their whole properties are strengthened). One gives rise to provoking change, the other to its control. The former is evident in the miniature's role of providing tentative solutions that are both suggestive and malleable; the latter is evident in the miniature's role of monitoring the designer's hierarchical decision making by determining, through its scale,

at what level of detail (whether pertaining to the whole or its parts) decisions can or should be made. As shall be seen, these twin roles are interrelated.

Miniatures and the Uses of Ambiguity

It was suggested before that design representations engage the perceptual processes of the designer because of their openness (incompleteness as representations). The lines of a plan of a house do not constitute a house. They only suggest a house and by the designer's inference become one. But there are degrees of incompleteness among representations, and in part the process of design can be understood as a sequence of calibrating these degrees. Early in the process, drawings generally have a relatively smaller scale. Schematic and diagrammatic plans and the like are common at this point. To the extent that these drawings are smaller, they are also more incomplete, and their use as design documents proceeds accordingly. The greater their degree of incompleteness, the greater the number of possible design solutions they can embody at one time. Particularly at the outset of the design process, when overly specific design representations might prematurely limit design options, a high level of incompleteness allows one representation to serve as a single substitute for a multitude of proposals. Gradually thereafter, as the process proceeds, ever-larger scaled representations are introduced. In the case of buildings, they might proceed from eight-inch and quarter-inch scale documents near the beginning to construction details and specifications at the end. Owing to their greater level of completeness, these later documents have the effect of gradually narrowing the range of possible interpretations of the design substitute, until finally (we hope) only one is possible: the eventual building.

In considering the capacity at the beginning of the process for architectural representations to support multiple interpretations, we should remember that, as with words, some drawings are also more imprecise than others. One drawing might be drawn with smeared soft charcoal and another with hard-line ink. Built on such observations, some architects have contrived ways of enhancing the suggestiveness of their early design representations. Many decline to use precise drawing tools at this time and prefer to do their early planning freehand. Others, like Louis Kahn, have even used crude tools such as unfixed vine charcoal on canary paper to give their early drawings a clouded and smeared imprecision.

As indicated earlier, properly calibrated at various points during the process, degrees of ambiguity are used in a dual role as a sort of perceptual *provocateur/contrôleur*. But this role of fostering both expansion and contraction of the solution search must not apply to only a single designer working alone. It also arises as a matter of course in the architect-client relationship and whenever a number of employees or a number of clients are involved in a single project. Drawings

and other representations must serve such groups as vehicles to form agreement. At the outset, they must be sufficiently broad to embody, juggle, and consolidate the ideas and aspirations of multiple interests, some of which may be mutually contradictory. At the end, they must be sufficiently precise to form the basis for legally binding contracts.

Miniatures and Closure

It has been stated that the miniatures used by designers are more open than their references and that this characteristic endows them with a capacity to support the sort of changes to a reference that are, after all, the business of design. At the same time, it was suggested that miniatures also contribute to the designer's ability to control that change. In passing, it was hinted that it might have something to do with miniatures controlling the perceptual stability of their references by also being more closed or stabile than those references.

A necessary condition of perception in daily life is that, at any point, we must assume the stability of the parts or subsystems of whatever we perceive. To perceive a face is to assume, at the same time, that its individual parts (eyes, ears, nose, and mouth) are stable and to proceed on the basis of what these parts form together, the face before us. In the moment that we cease to assume the stability of any one of the parts—say by noticing the color of the eyes—we are in the position of perceiving that part as the object of our at-

tention and are no longer perceiving the face. What is true of these instances is also true of our perceptions and, I might add, our intentions with respect to design drawings. In drawing a site plan, an architect is concerned with the relationships between the buildings, not with the individual buildings. Likewise, a detail of a door frame is concerned with the fit between the parts, such as the door post and head, not the molecular structure of the wood of these parts. A drawing can embody relationships at a number of hierarchical levels, but, at any given point in the design process, our consideration of a drawing must of necessity assume the stability of the parts of the design and place only the relationships between those parts at issue.

We must at the same time observe that things are not as simple as these last paragraphs would suggest. Although we cannot destabilize the parts of anything in our attention without also destabilizing our attention, it remains a fact of life that we are still free at any point to shift our attention and consider those very parts, and we do this constantly. Our perceptual and mental processes are con-

[5] For these reasons alone, it should not be surprising that representation includes many miniatures but few *maxiatures*. Those few *maxiatures* we do encounter are usually those, such as the models of chemists and material scientists, that relate information that would otherwise remain subsensory.

[6] J. B. S. Haldane, "On Being the Right Size," in *World of Mathematics*, Vol. 2, (New York: Simon and Schuster, 1956) pp. 952-957.

stantly plying and ranging over the hierarchies of objects, concepts, and events. At one moment we consider a house and in the next moment its door. Our ability to roam the hierarchical scales of perception seemingly has no end. In the face of such riotous processes, we might ask what would possibly prevent designers from suffering a kind of constant affliction of wandering attention, even as they attend to their drawings. The answer will be found in the size of those drawings.

There is an amusing sculpture of a baboon that Picasso once made for one of his children[7] that toys precisely with these questions of subsystem stability[8] and size. For our purposes, the interest of this piece lies in the control it exerts in delaying our tendency to destabilize subparts. The head of this baboon is actually made from a tinplate toy car, and the intrigue of this piece lies in the fact that we do not immediately notice this car. Instead, as Picasso knew would be the case, we are so occupied with seeing the baboon that we are at first unable to see its parts and their subparts (head, and then eyes, ears, nose etc.). It is only after studying the piece for a while that we are able to destabilize the piece to the point that we observe that the eyes and mouth grinning at us are actually the headlights and front grill of a toy automobile. At least for a few moments—and therein lies the charm of this piece—the subsystems of Picasso's baboon are stable. The question is, How did Picasso know we would see this piece in this way?

It has not yet been mentioned that there is a point beyond which our perceptual processes must cease to break things into ever smaller parts: that point at which, owing to its small size, the parts of a thing must remain subsensory.[9] And at sizes approaching this barrier, there are also conditions of reduced tendency, which, as Picasso's baboon demonstrates, can be used masterfully to specific effect. Conditioned on the size of the toy car of which it was fashioned, Picasso's baboon was roughly one-eighth the size of the real thing. At that size, he could rest assured that our tendency would be to see the baboon first and to scrutinize its face only later. But he did also want us to eventually notice those parts. That, after all, was his joke. So he made the baboon small enough to delay destabilization but not so small as to preclude it.

Likewise, at their even smaller size relative to the reference, the scales of architectural miniatures are precisely calibrated to delimit the hierarchical level at which inquiry should proceed. By predetermining the sizes at which things are shown through the use of scales, the agenda is already set as to which things we can and should attend (those things that at that scale we can easily destabilize) and likewise those we should not (those we cannot). A one-sixteenth-inch to one foot plan addresses questions of overall room organization, but leaves questions of exact window and door location unanswered and, equally important, unasked. Similarly, a one-eighth-inch to one-foot plan answers questions of

exact window and door location but leaves unanswered questions of their detail.

The interdependence of design issues and scale is a question of both craft and perception. The issue of the material of a wall, for example, goes unanswered at a scale of one-sixteenth-inch to the foot, partly because material cannot be represented at that scale. Our drawing skills are simply insufficient to allow us to draw one-sixteenth scale wood or concrete. Moreover, since at that scale the two closely spaced lines we might have drawn to indicate a wall seem a relatively satisfying and complete substitute for a wall, the question of the wall's material does not even occur to us. It would, however, occur at a scale of one inch to the foot. At that scale, not only would we be able to draw materials but also leaving out such details would cause our drawing to appear empty. Unless fleshed out such a drawing would seem too large for its content. It would solicit answers about material because it would also beg the question.

Moving in and Stepping Back

It has already been stated that there is an apparent paradox about miniatures. While they are less complete than their references and their incompleteness allows for the kind of openness of interpretation that propels the process of design, we have observed, at the same time, that they are also more complete than their references. We have observed that this characteristic, by masking small scaled subparts from scrutiny, also gains some measure of control over the very process of design that miniaturization initiates in the first place. At the same time, however, we must observe that the process of designing is never quite so neat as might be suggested by a hierarchical progression moving smoothly from small scale schematics to large scale details and from general ideas to which all will aspire to contract documents that all will sign. This after all was the description of the overly simplistic *analysis-synthesis* model. Design is messier, and decisions are made at many levels of detail throughout the process. In fact, much as is suggested by the *concept test* model, architects work at multiple levels throughout the process. Though the general progress of design may proceed from smaller-scale to ever larger-scale documents, at any point along the way other scales are in consistent use. Architects, after all, are responsible for the making of objects. Many, if not most, of their concerns exist at a level of detailed construction. They cannot afford to remain above such decisions for too long.

My wise painting instructor had known this to be true of painting. And so, when he advised us to keep a consistent level of incompleteness across the entire face, he also advised that, whenever we made a decision relative to a part (a potentially upsetting decision), we should refer that decision back to the whole face. We should do this, he suggested, by frequently stepping back from our canvas in order to gain a more distant view.

We should do this even as we moved in, speaking figuratively, in developing the portrait in ever greater detail. In essence he was recommending a *bottom-up* strategy that should be used in tandem with a *top-down* strategy. As with architects, he was urging us to burn the candle at both ends. And as used by architects, he was advocating a strategy of representation that would light the match, allow both ends to burn, and control the fire as well.

---

[7] E. H. Gombrich, *Art and Illusion*, p. 104.

[8] The concept of subsystem stability is presented in Herbert A. Simon, *The Sciences of the Artificial*, (Cambridge: M.I.T. Press, 1969) p. 77.

[9] Beyond the capacity of our senses to apprehend e.g., with the naked eye, it is impossible to see the parts of a grain of sand.

Chapter 4

This chapter presents and discusses the projective techniques that underlie the drawing conventions of architects and designers. Because these explanations are lengthy and technical in character, they have to be balanced with simultaneous freehand drawing. For example, the exercises on the *office method* perspectives should be accompanied with exercises from the earlier section entitled *Freehand Perspective* in chapter 2. This is proposed not only to make the technical material more palatable but also, for its reciprocal effect, to guide that freehand drawing with the technical knowledge of this chapter. As a first step in this process, the exercises within this chapter are accompanied with adjacent freehand exercises. We will begin with orthographic projection and from there proceed to paraline and perspective projection.

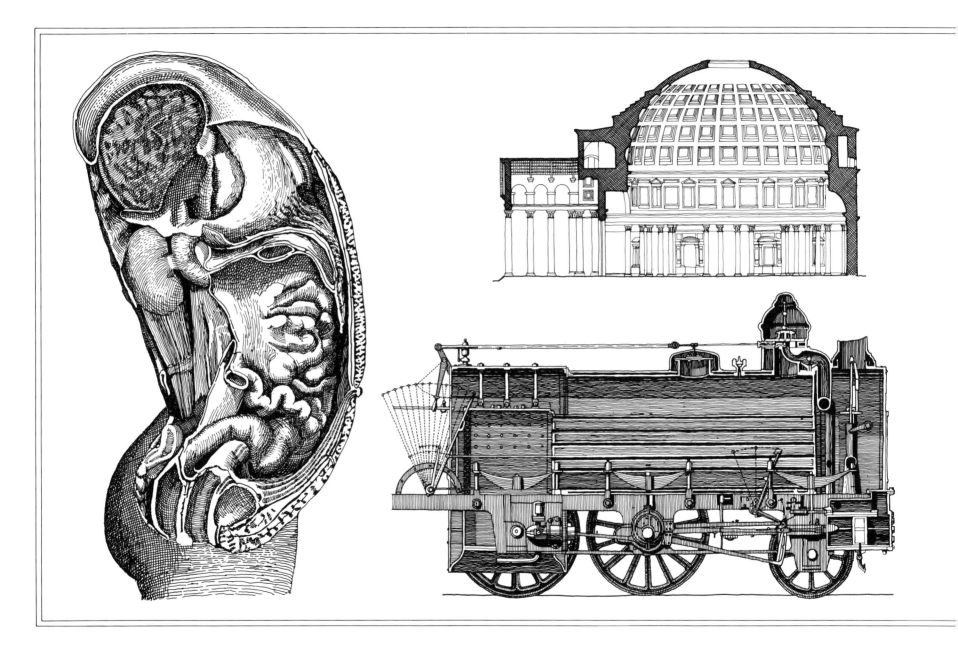

ORTHOGRAPHIC PROJECTION

Orthographic projection includes the set of drawings, plans, elevations, and sections we most commonly associate with architects. Despite today's wider definition of roles in practice, as the document of choice for the contract documents from which buildings are built, these drawings still constitute the central product of most architects. There are two attributes of orthographic drawings that make them useful to their roles within practice:

1) *They are drawn to scale and without distortion of shape.* This fact contributes to the process of design in two ways. One is perceptual. It concerns the contribution of scale to the provocation and control of design process. The other is regulatory. Scaled documents are used to control the size, configuration, and placement of elements in construction.

2) *They are limited to single aspects.* They are able to show only a part of a building at one time, as when an elevation shows only the front. While it is a problem of sorts for their usage (they must, as a consequence, be combined in one's mind to create an understanding of the whole) this limitation also serves to delimit the number of issues that have to be addressed at any given time to a manageable number.

Figure 135. *A Gallery of Orthographic Views* (after views from *The Complete Encyclopedia of Illustration,* and *A History of Architecture on the Comparative Method).*

ORTHOGRAPHIC PROJECTION

As distinct from perspective projection (which has already been discussed in chapter 2 and will be taken up again later in this chapter), orthographic projection presents a boundless and unlocalized field of vision. Unlike perspective views, orthographic views do *not* show the view from any one position in space. Rather, they show the view from an infinite set of positions. Thinking of an orthographic view as a view from a wall of eyes would be closer to an understanding of its optics.

Two rules govern orthographic projection:

1) At least one spatial axis of the viewed object (its height, length, or width) is parallel to the picture plane. In practice, usually two spatial axes, or one face such as a top or front, are parallel to the picture plane.

2) The viewed object is projected to the picture plane exclusively with orthogonal sight lines (lines that intersect the picture plane at 90°).

Because they represent only one aspect of an object, a single orthographic view usually cannot present a complete sense of an object. Consequently, orthographic views are rarely used singly. Rather, they are used in tandem with other orthographic views of the same object.

Figure 136. *Orthographic Projection.* Orthographic views are projected at 90° to the picture plane and show only one aspect of the object.

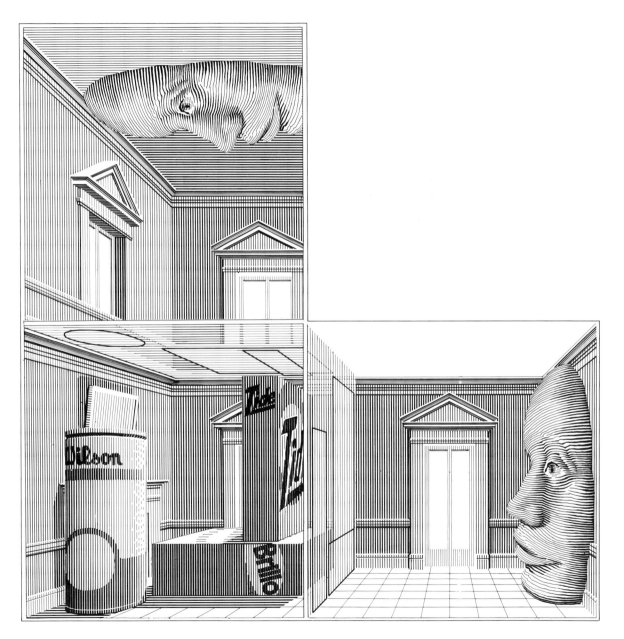

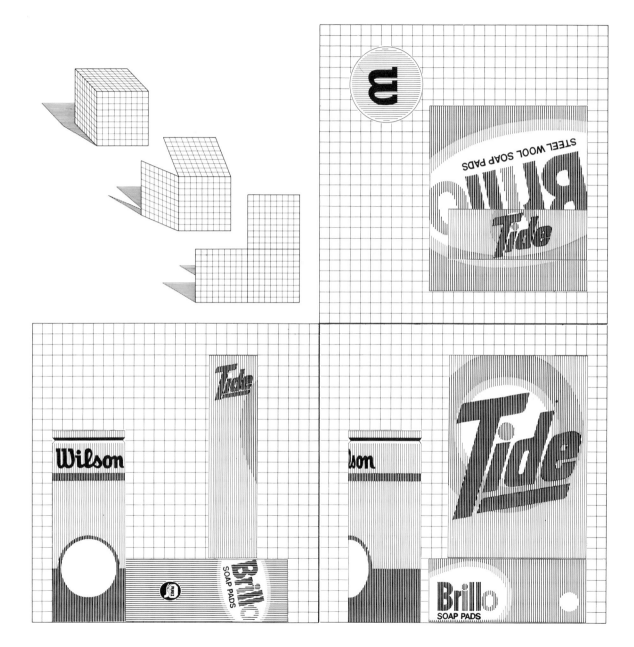

Commonly, at least three orthographic views from three different directions are needed to give an adequate description of an object. They include plans (downward-looking views of the top or inside floor of an object), elevations (upright views of the front or side of an object), and sections (upright views of the interior of an object).

The task of reuniting the several orthographic views of the several aspects of an object is left to the viewer, often without explanation. This task is not always easy. Ideally the several views are positioned relative to one another such that their relationship, both to each other and to the original object, is clearly implied.

Figure 137. *Multi Viewing.* Commonly several views are used in tandem.

Plans

Plans are downward looking, normal ortho-graphic views. There are two kinds of plans: floor plans and roof plans. The position of the picture plane relative to the viewed object distinguishes the one kind from the other.

1) *Roof plan or top view:* A roof plan is a view from above. It is generated by projecting an image of an object up to a picture plane which has been positioned above and outside that viewed object.

2) *Floor plan:* A floor plan is a sectional view. It is generated by projecting an image of an object up to a horizontal picture plane that has been inserted into that object. Floor plans always distinguish cut-through material (material touching the inserted picture plane) from viewed material (material below the picture plane).

Among orthographic views, plans are the least perceptual but the most conceptual. In that they view the visual world in a downward-looking direction, they relate only circum-stantially to our normal upright sense of the world. Moreover, in cutting through the in-sides and outsides of objects and in showing a boundless breadth of field, they seem to violate a normal sense of time and place.

Figure 138. *Roof Plan and Floor Plan.*

128

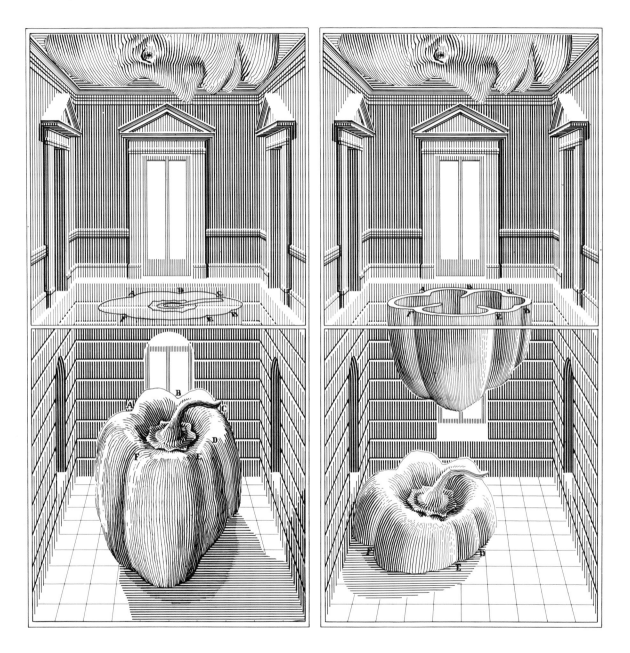

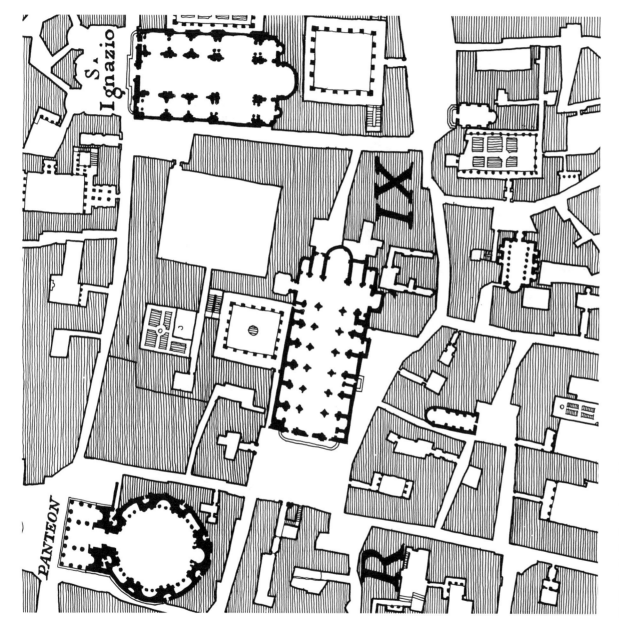

Yet plans do seem familiar in another way that reflects the environment in which we live. Because of gravity and because we also live on the earth's surface, most of the things we see in daily life tend to be positioned on the ground. Thus chairs, tables, buildings, roads, and the like tend to be located in our minds according to the ground's coordinates. In that they replicate that same ground surface, plans reflect our mental map of the world.[10]

In practice, plans are used to show: 1) the location, length, thickness, and material of walls and columns; 2) the location, depth, and width of wall openings; 3) floor and ground material; 4) the location, length, and width of rooms; 5) the location of fixtures (sinks, lights, outlets, etc.); 6) horizontal circulation; and 7) the location of adjacent structures.

Figure 139. *Plan of Rome* (after *Nolli Plan*).

---

[10] This characteristic of plans (that they align with our mental map of the world) is at the root of the usage of *upward position in the visual field* as the central pictorial cue of early childhood drawings. In effect, such drawings are elevations combined with plans. The elevations provide the visual profile, and the plans provide the location. For a detailed discussion of upward position in the visual field, see pp. 58–59.

Elevations

Elevations are horizontal orthographic views. They are generated by projecting an image of an object out to a vertical picture plane that is positioned outside the object.

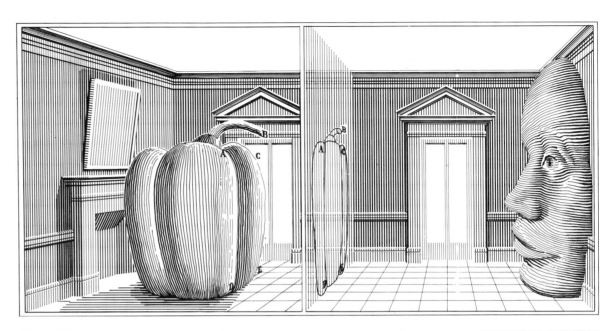

Figure 140. *Elevation.*

Because they mimic our normal upright viewing of the world and because they are not sectional views, among orthographic views elevations offer the closest semblance to the appearance of the objects they represent. In practice elevations are used to show: 1) the height, width, and material of walls and roofs; 2) the location, dimension, and nature of wall openings; and 3) the appearance of a building.

Figure 141. *Elevation of Design Project* (project under direction of Professor Arne Larson). Robert Herscoe.

130

Sections

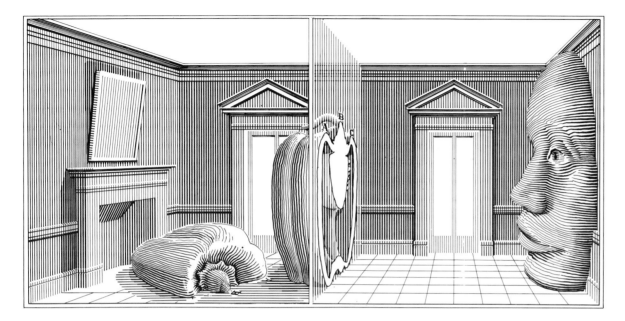

Sections are horizontal orthographic views of sectioned or cut objects. They are generated by projecting an image of an object out to a vertical picture plane that has been inserted into the object. Like plans, sections always distinguish cut-through material (material that is cut through by the insertion of the picture plane) from viewed material. Because they are cut along a building's vertical axis, the plane along which gravity is resisted, sections offer the clearest information about structure. Such questions as load-bearing materials, method of joining, method of spanning, width of spanning, and depth of spanning are the business of the section.

Figure 142. *Section.*

Sections combine the conceptual qualities of plans with the perceptual qualities of elevations: like plans, they position us inside and outside; like elevations, they mimic our normal upright viewing of an object. Sections show: 1) the location, height, thickness, and material of walls and columns; 2) the location, height, and depth of wall openings; 3) the location, thickness, span, material, and connection of floors, beams and roofs; 4) the location, height, and width of rooms; 5) the location, thickness, width, and depth of foundations; and 6) vertical circulation.

Figure 143. *Sectional View of Soldiers and Sailor's Memorial, Pittsburgh* (project under direction of Professor Robert S. Taylor). John Krusienski.

The following set of exercises is directed at building understanding of orthographic documents on the basis of spatial understandings that were introduced in the first chapter of the book in *Mass and Volume* (pp. 18-37). The focus of these exercises upon volume as a figural element is critical to the student's ability to project the third dimension into the making and reading of these documents. The first of these exercises uses the same system of representing volume as was used in that earlier set.

ORTHOGRAPHIC PROJECTION
Exercise 1
Section

With charcoal tone in a sectional view, describe the depth of the volume within a building. Where the volume is deep, draw more. Where the volume is shallow, draw less. Try to bring to this exercise two characteristics from your earlier work in the first chapter: a sense of depth, as in *The Volume Between* (see p. 35), and a sense of occupancy, as in *The Volume Within* (see p. 36).

Materials: Carbon pencil, cold-press illustration board. This exercise can be applied to plan views as well as sectional views.

Figure 144. Joseph Romano.
Figure 145. (opposite page) Rick Marron.

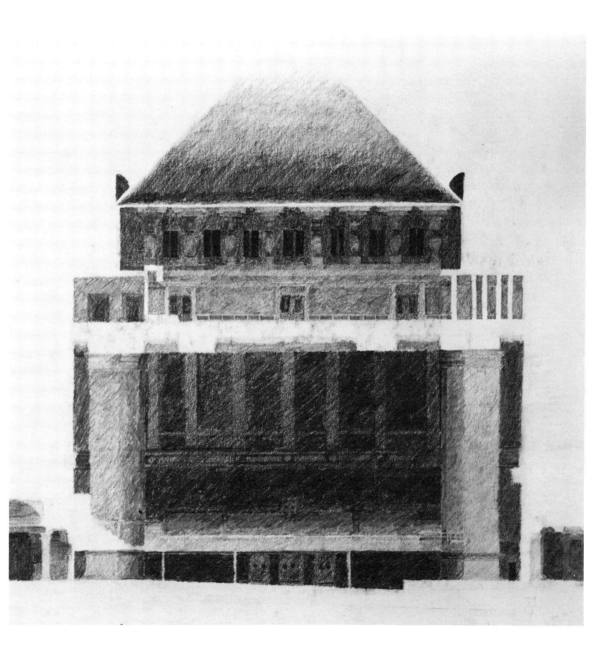

133

ORTHOGRAPHIC PROJECTION
Exercise 2
Elevation

Like the previous exercise, this exercise also seeks to build understanding of orthographic projection on the basis of spatial under-standings that were introduced in the first chapter of the book in *Mass and Volume* (pp. 18-37). In this exercise, however, a slightly different system of representation is used. Whereas the previous exercises called only for a process of darkening those areas that were farther away (in effect, considering the page as representing a foreground of sorts), in this drawing the page, which is neutral gray in tone, is understood as something which can be both darkened to produce an effect of greater depth or lightened (pulled forward, as it were) to produce an effect of greater nearness.

Another aspect of this exercise, its choreog-raphy as a group exercise, arises in under-standings of the optics of orthographic pro-jection that were previously presented. It has been stated that orthographic projection presents a boundless and unlocalized field of vision, and that, unlike perspective views, they do *not* show the view from any one position. Rather, they show the view from an

Figure 146. *Facade of S. Gilles.* First Year Group Project co-taught with Jill Watson. The class Included: Hajime Ando, Nick Arauz, Lisa Aufman, Ben Bell, Colin Brice, Scott Chiang, Michael Gallin, Nicholas Hague, Kenneth Kim, Judy Lee, Peter McLaughlin, Alan Mizuki, Richard Monopoli, Michael O' Sullivan, Michael Parris, Basil Richardson, Sean Starkweather, Zaidi Tuah.

infinite set of positions. This exercise manifests the unlocalized character of orthographic projection by distributing the task of drawing over a broader set of positions in space, in this case over the number of members of the class.

As would be the case with all such composite group murals (not just one with this specialized content), this assignment has an important side benefit beyond the product per se. The students teach each other without the instructor's having to intervene in any way. Merely through adjacencies of better students working next to weaker students, stronger and more focused thinking begins to enter into the work of the weaker students as a consequence of their trying to maintain a seamless appearance across the whole drawing. This exercise is a case of the whole being greater than the sum of the parts.

The assignment As a class project, represent the depth of volume in front of a facade. Use ebony pencil and white Prismacolor drawn with a consistant angular stroke on gray chipboard to render a highly atmospheric effect.

Materials: Ebony pencil, white Prismacolor, chipboard.

ORTHOGRAPHIC PROJECTION
Project
Plan, Section, Elevation.

What follows presents a design project of the character I have given from time to time in second-year design studios. It is included in this volume as a demonstration of a design application of the exercises immediately preceding and of those on volume from chapter 1 (see *Volume Exercises 1-6,* pp. 32-37). Like those exercises, this project treats volume as the figural element of composition from the start and is more generally directed at fostering an understanding of orthographic projection that would go beyond materiality. The instrument of this understanding is the project's requirement that the building be generated by a process of eroding or subtracting volume as distinct from one of producing built material.

The drawing techniques used throughout the project are the same as those in *Exercise 1* and *Exercise 2* of this section. They are intended to support continuing attention to volume as a figural issue of drawing and, relatedly, to support a sense of designing through a process of subtraction. Both are deemed important as a basis for the space-making activity that is at the very heart of what an architect does. Several characteristics of these projects deserve mentioning:

1) The beginning condition of the project is an assumed preexisting limestone monolith that occupies the entire potential volume of the site. At the outset, in effect, solid material is maximized (it is everywhere), and more importantly free volume is minimized (it is nowhere to be found). It is worth pointing this out because this is the exact opposite of what is the case in most design problems. As a consequence, all occupied volume is generated from the direction of its minimal possible size (there is none until such time as it is designed into existence), rather than, as is customary, from the direction of its maximum possible size (it is everywhere until such time as it is shaped by walls, floors, and roofs). In this way, the important question of the minimal volume required for a given programmed activity is made more accessible to address.

2) Since form is generated by making volume rather than by making material, volume automatically becomes the more obvious figure of the design.

3) In a manner discussed with respect to Nicholaides in chapter 1 and discussed at length in chapter 3, this exercise gives considerable support to the idea of having the activity of drawing be analogous in some essential way to the activity that it represents. In this project creating volume is the activity that is represented. Likewise, in the activity of drawing the charcoal means and represents the volume that is being made to be occupied.

4) To the extent that material continues to be the figural element (figure-ground reversals are often unavoidable), this project supports the fundamentally optimistic assumption that the project's solution already materially exists. Though the task involves a monumental amount of editing, it is still just that: editing. Nothing new needs to be manufactured. Only that which would not apply needs to be removed.

The project The project shown at right used a ceramics cooperative for its program. It assumed a limestone monolith 30' high x 120' wide x 160' deep in a warehouse district in Los Angeles.

Figure 147. (opposite page) *Ceramics Cooperative.* Patrick Sutton.

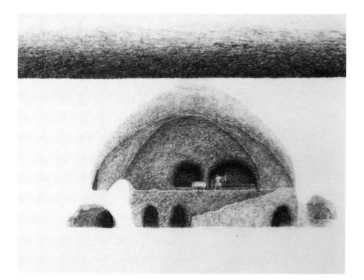

137

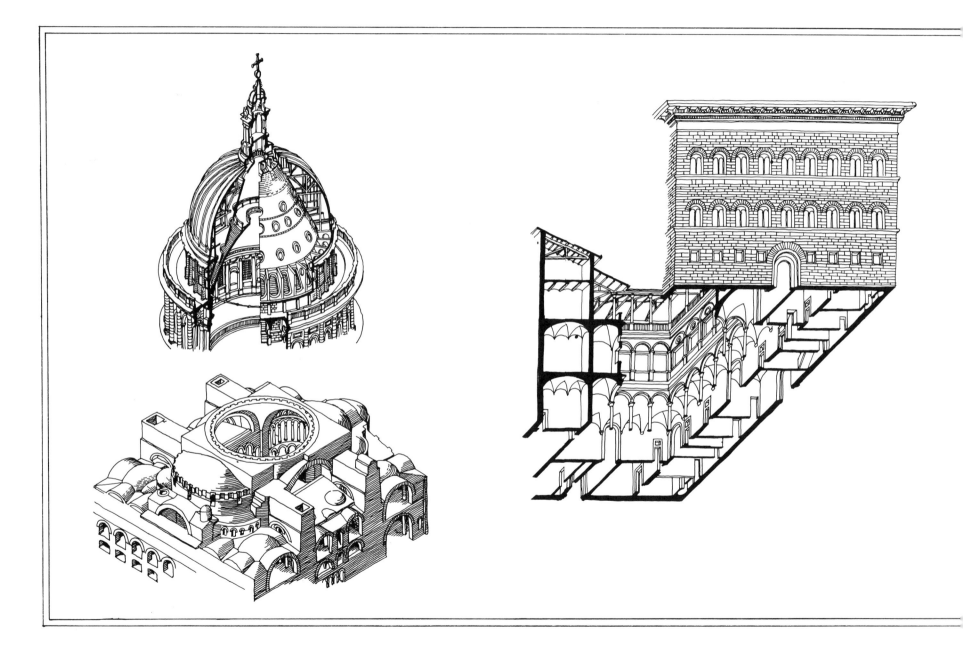

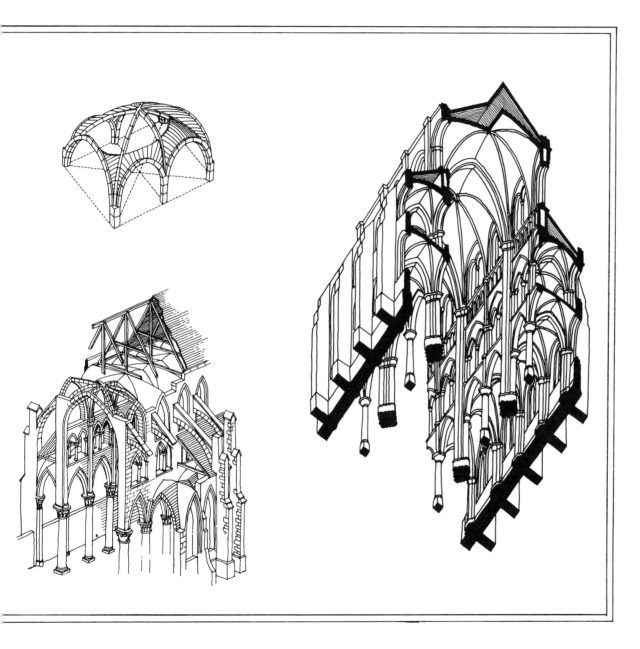

PARALINE VIEWS

Like orthographic views, paraline views provide scaled representations of objects and show a boundless and unlocalized field of vision. But unlike their relative and because they show objects from inclined angles, paraline views show three faces of objects in one view. There are two categories of paraline views: axonometric and oblique. Though each is projected differently, their use is so much alike that it seems best to speak of them together. As a practical matter, the only important difference between them is that oblique views can be generated off plans and elevations because of the procedure of their projection, by which one face remains parallel to the picture plane.

Both offer a powerful sense of constructing an object in three dimensions on the page. Owing to the paired characteristics of showing all three dimensions and being drawn to scale, one can treat these drawings as a form of assembly. As is explained in the exercises at the end of this section, this sense of drawing as assembly can be supported by two instruments:
1) learning paraline views initially on the computer (where it is my experience they are best learned) and 2) using freehand exercises that require the mechanical movement of parts. The discussion will begin with the topic of the optics of the two categories of paraline views: axonometic and oblique.

Figure 148. *A Gallery of Paraline Views* (after views from *A History of Architecture on the Comparative Method*).

Axonometric Projection

Two rules govern axonometric views and distinguish them from oblique views: 1) The viewed object is tilted relative to the picture plane. 2) The viewed object is projected to the picture place exclusively with orthogonal sight lines, lines that intercept the picture plane at an angle of 90°, a rule they share with orthographic views.

Figure 149. *Axonometric Projection*. In axonometric projection, the object is tilted relative to the picture plane but it is projected to it with orthogonals.

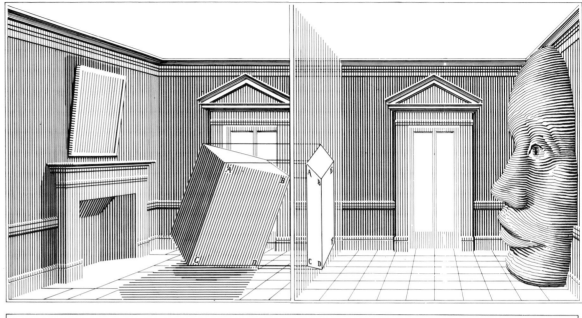

Though projected differently, axonometric views share the following characteristics with oblique views: 1) All lines, corners, and edges that are parallel in fact are parallel in the axonometric view. 2) All lines, corners, and edges that are parallel to one of the object's three spatial axes can be drawn to scale.

Figure 150. *Axonometric Projection*.

140

Oblique Projection

Two rules govern oblique views and distinguish them from axonometric views: 1) One face of the viewed object is always parallel to the picture plane. 2) The viewed object is projected to the picture plane with oblique sight lines (lines that intercept the picture plane at angles other than 90°).

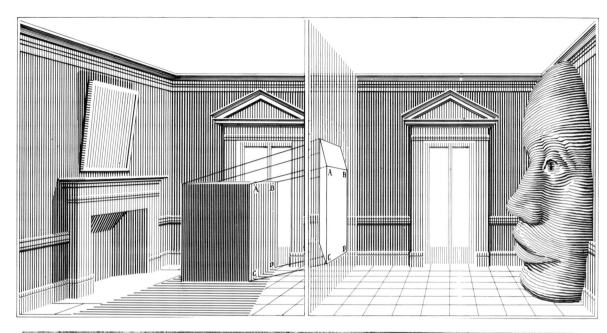

Figure 151. *Oblique Projection.* In oblique projection, the object is positioned normal to the picture plane, but it is projected to it at an angle other than 90°.

Though projected differently, oblique views share the following characteristics with axonometric views: 1) All lines, corners, and edges that are parallel in fact are parallel in the oblique view. 2) All lines, corners, and edges that are parallel to one of the object's three spatial axes can be drawn to scale.

Unique to oblique views, because it remains parallel to the picture plane, one face can be drawn without distortion of shape. This characteristic is of great convenience since for this reason they can be generated from plans and elevations

Figure 152. *Lady Wenji's Return to China,* 12th c.
Denman Waldo Ross Collection
Courtesy, Museum of Fine Arts, Boston.

Axonometric Projection

Two kinds of axonometric views are commonly used: isometry and dimetry. The tilt of the object relative to the picture plane distinguishes them.

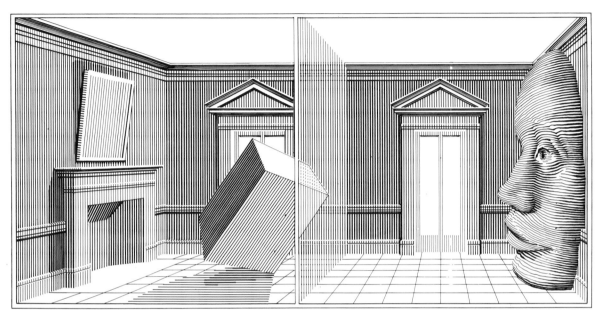

Isometric projection   Isometric views tilt the object such that its three spatial axes intercept the picture plane at equal angles.   Figure 153.

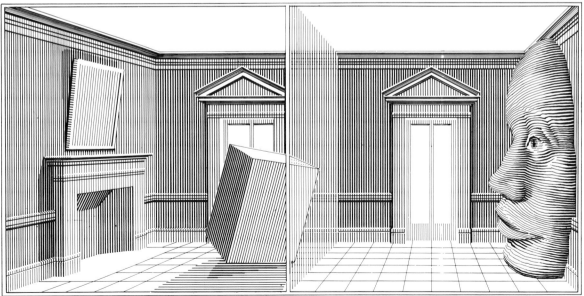

Dimetric projection   Dimetric views orient the object such that two of its three spatial axes intercept the picture plane at equal angles.   Figure 154.

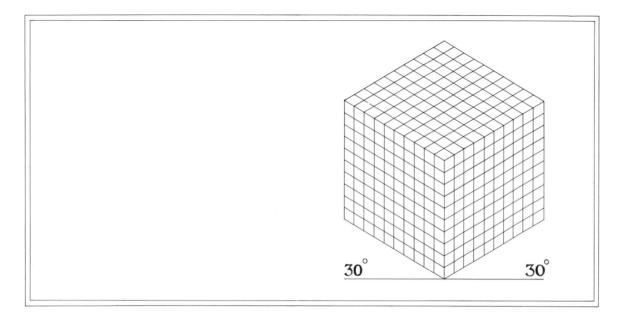

30°   30°

Isometric projection As a consequence of their orientation relative to the picture plane, isometric views have the following characteristics: 1) The angles between the represented x, y, and z axes are equal in the drawing; they all equal 120°. 2) The three faces are equally distorted. 3) Lengths along the x, y, and z axes are measured at full scale. No compensatory foreshortening is used. Figure 155.

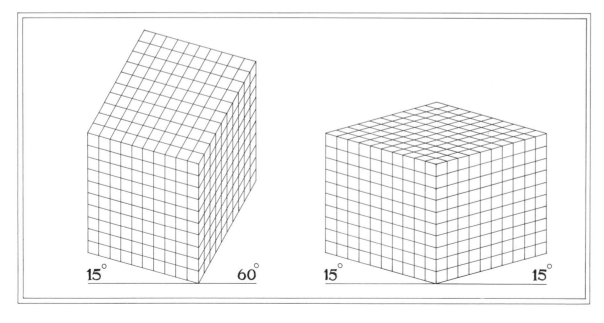

15°   60°   15°   15°

Dimetric projection As a consequence of their orientation relative to the picture plane, dimetric views have the following characteristics: 1) Two of the three angles between the represented x, y, and z axes are equal in the drawing. 2) Two of the three faces are distorted equally. 3) Lengths along the spatial axes can be foreshortened where appropriate. Two typical dimetric setups are shown at left. Figure 156.

143

Oblique Projection

There are two kinds of oblique views: plan oblique and elevation oblique. The face parallel to the picture plane (top or front) distinguishes one kind from the other.

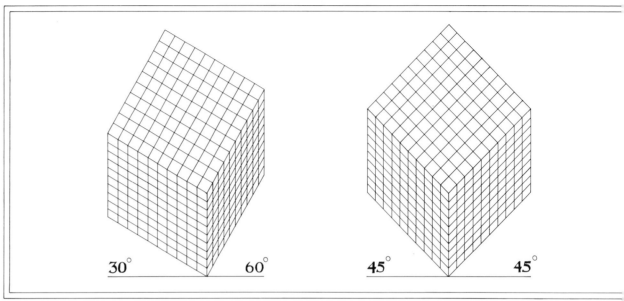

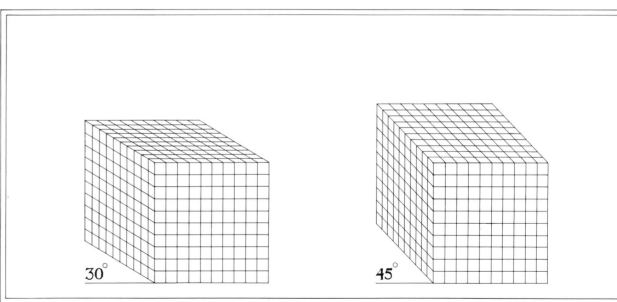

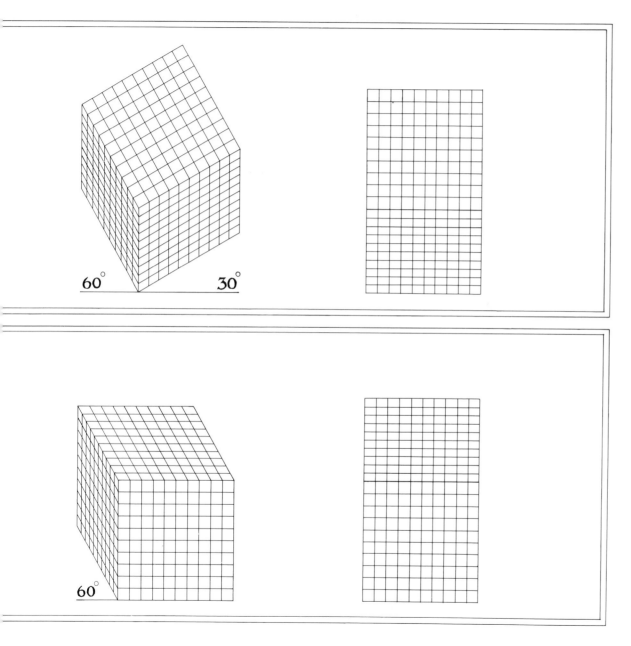

60°   30°

Plan oblique Plan oblique views orient the object such that its top is parallel to the picture plane.
Figure 157.

60°

Elevation oblique Elevation oblique views orient the object such that its front is parallel to the picture plane. Figure 158.

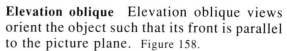

PARALINE PROJECTION
Exercise 1
Computer-Generated Paraline Views

It was stated at the beginning of this section that paraline views characteristically embody a sense of constructing an object in three dimensions on the page. It is my experience that students gain the most essential understanding of this sense if they learn paraline views initially on the computer. Doing so offers a procedural analogy to construction that assists this understanding. At the start, the x, y, z coordinate grid is understood appropriately as a background abstraction rather than as a construction. Then (and this is where the mechanical analogy is served) individual lines are dragged with a mouse into positions within that grid. The sense that one is engaged in an activity quite like the construction of a *jungle gym* or a similar framework is so unmistakable that understanding proceeds effortlessly.

The reader should remember that the idea that drawing should provide a mechanical analogy to the object is at the heart of the Nicholaides-inspired exercises presented in chapter 1 and at the heart of chapter 3. Though this is basically a volume about freehand drawing, I have included the computer-generated image at right for its relevance to this recurring theme.

Figure 159. *Nine Square Grid Problem.* Ted Terranova. From "computer modeling" and "introduction to architecture" classes taught by Bruce Lindsey, Paul Rosenblatt, and Rob Woodbury.

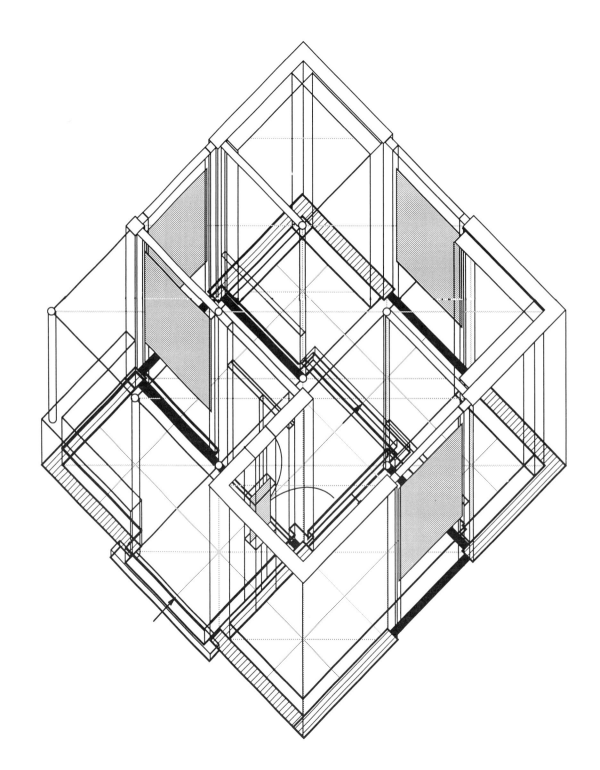

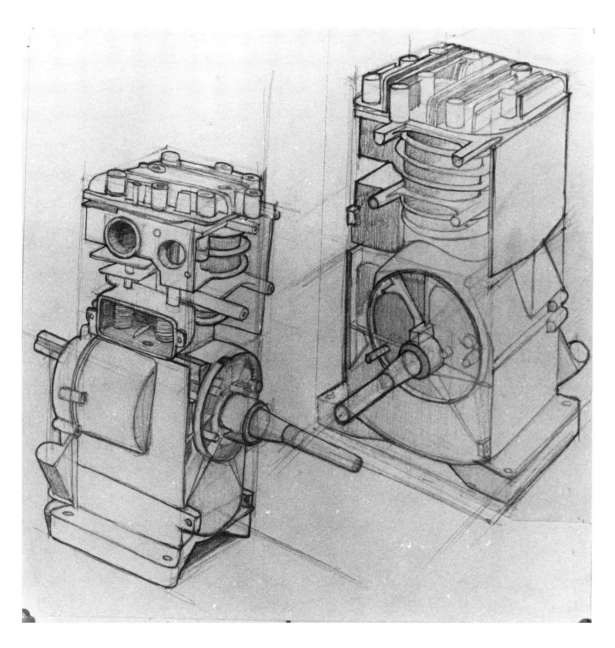

Exercise 2
Axonometric Projection
Sequential Views of Machine Parts

Subjects for paraline views should have clear and interesting geometries. Machine parts, lawn mower engines, motorcycle engines, and the like are ideal.

Execute a series of axonometric drawings that show moving around a machine part. Begin by establishing a set of generating lines of geometry. These should be light but freehand. They should fix the overall x, y, z coordinates on which the drawing will be based. Then build the object as an instance of that geometry.

Materials: Ebony pencil, bond paper.

Figure 160. Susan Helwig.

PARALINE PROJECTION
Exercise 3
Axonometric Projection
How an Engine Fits Together

The intention of this view is to build on the sort of drawings that are usually included in automotive manuals, and it should be executed in that spirit. As in the previous exercise, it is important throughout that there be a clear unmistakable sense of constructing with geometry.

Execute one axonometric drawing that shows the construction of an engine. Begin by establishing a set of generating lines of geometry that are light but freehand. They should fix the overall x, y, z coordinates and axial relationships on which the drawing will be based. Then build the engine as an instance of that geometry.

Materials: Ebony pencil, bond paper.

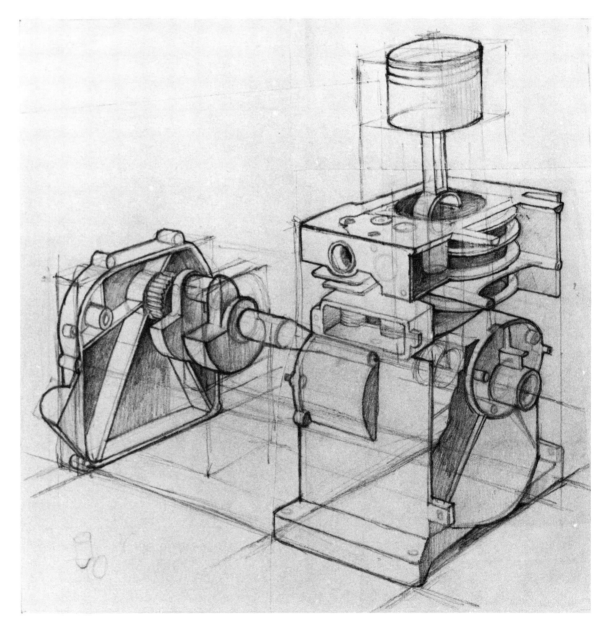

Figure 161. Susan Helwig.

It was pointed out earlier that oblique projection allows the possibility of generating the view directly from an orthographic view. This owed to the fact that oblique views are projected with one face of the object remaining parallel to the picture plane. The following project, which is built off a plan, uses this possibility as its point of departure. It was also stated that, in contrast to perspectives, which have a delimited breadth of field and a defined position of view, paraline views have a boundless and unlocalized field of vision. They present a clear direction of viewing, but they show that view from what amounts to an infinite number of positions. The following project uses this fact as a point of departure by spreading the view over several sheets of paper, in effect broadening the station point.

Begin by selecting a major hall, the nave of a church, for example. Then, at a large size and over several sheets of taped-together bond paper, lightly represent the plan as it would appear if viewed from the basement. Then, through that plan project the hall as it would appear when you look up. As you draw, try to maintain a clear sense of construction. Draw the geometry first and the architecture second as an instance of that geometry.

Materials: Ebony pencil, bond paper.

Figure 162. Azizan Aziz.

PARALINE PROJECTION
Exercise 5
Oblique Projection
Paper Doll Drawings

Earlier the point was made that paraline views characteristically embody a sense of actually constructing an object in three dimensions on the page. Like the first exercise in this section, the following exercise is also analogous to this same sense of actual construction, though its relationship is more mechanical. It offers yet one more instance of a treatment of drawing as an act of making, an idea first introduced in discussions of Nicholaides and developed elsewhere, notably in chapter 3.

Here the analogy arises in the treatment of drawn objects. Objects are first drawn, then they are Xeroxed, then they are cut out, and then they are finally assembled together into one composition like the individual pieces of clothing on a paper doll. This exercise builds on the twin characteristics of paraline drawings, namely, that they represent objects to scale and show three faces of objects.

The exercise Using paraline drawings to make Xeroxed paper cutouts, generate an assembled paraline world.

Figure 163. *Altar.* Douglas Cooper, 1984, carbon pencil on paper, 96" x 96" (private collection). This view was developed from the Xeroxed assemblage shown on the opposite page.

Figure 164. (opposite page) *Altar.* (detail from Xerox underdrawing).

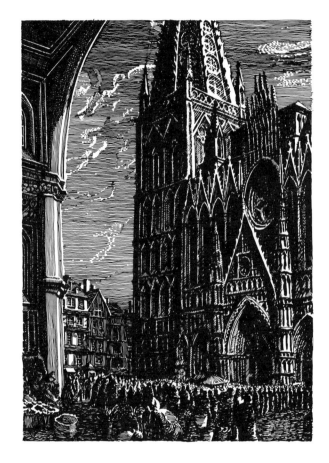

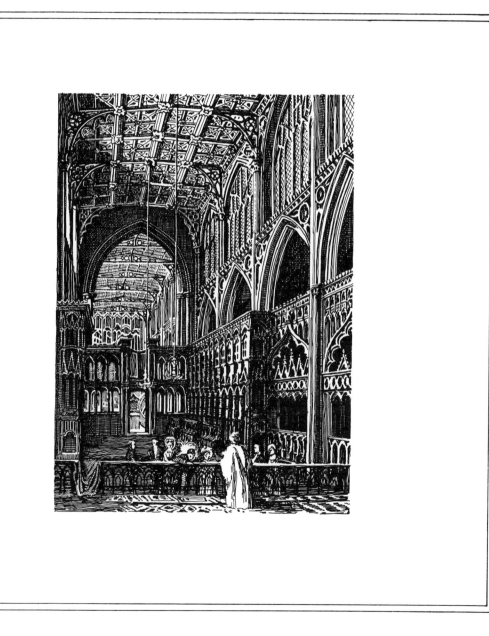

PERSPECTIVE PROJECTION

At this point, we return to a subject we have already considered at some length in chapter 2. Perspective was discussed in that chapter largely as a question of freehand drawing and in its relationship to vision. Appropriate to this chapter, here it will be addressed as an issue of projective geometry.

Perspective projection is a system of drawing that provides a representation of the momentary appearance of a scene from a single position in space. Though they may be generated from scaled orthographic representations, perspective views themselves do not provide an accurate measure of the objects they show. They are not usable as measured drawings. They do, however, offer a capability beyond those of other drawing systems. Because they represent the view from a single position in space, perspective views (unlike normal orthographic, axonometric, or oblique views) are able to show the appearance of an interior space.

Figure 165. *A Gallery of Perspective Views* (after views from *The Complete Encyclopedia of Illustration*).

153

PERSPECTIVE PROJECTION

Two rules govern perspective projection: 1) The viewed object is projected to or through the picture plane with sight lines that converge at the station point (the assumed position of the viewer's eye). 2) The picture plane is perpendicular to the line of sight (the direction in which the viewer is looking).

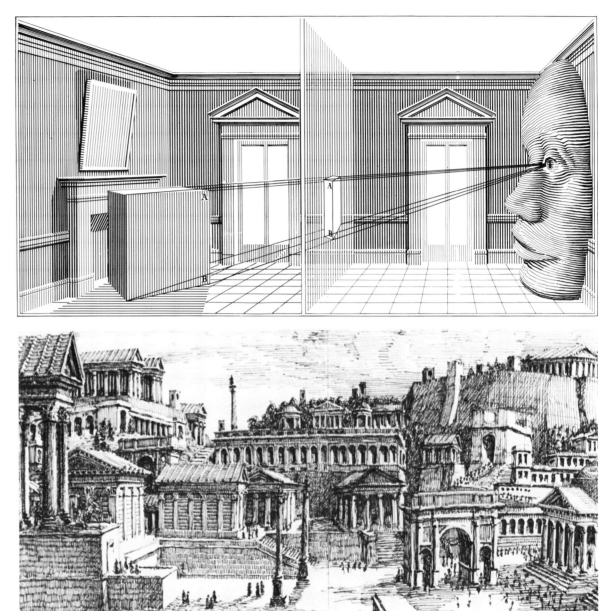

Figure 166. *Geometry of Perspective Projection.*

Perspective views have the following characteristics: 1) Lines, corners, and edges that are parallel in fact are parallel in the perspective view only if they are also parallel to the picture plane. Otherwise they converge at common points (vanishing points). 2) Lines, corners, edges, and planes that are parallel to the picture plane can be drawn to scale only if they lie flat on the picture plane. Otherwise their size must be determined with the use of measuring lines. 3) Angles and planer shapes can be drawn without distortion of shape only if they are parallel to the picture plane. 4) The image size of objects diminishes with greater distance from the viewer (the station point).

Figure 167. *Perspective Projection.*

154

Unlike normal orthographic, axonometric, and oblique views, perspective views do not represent a boundless and unlocalized visual field. Rather, they approximate the view from a singular position in space: 1) They approximate its visual overlaps. 2) They approximate its array of highlight, half-light, shade, and shadow. 3) They approximate its atmospheric effects (see "Pictorial Depth Cues, Aerial Perspective," p. 66). 4) They approximate its image foreshortening. 5) They approximate its image diminution (see "Pictorial Depth Cues, Size Perspective," p. 64).

Figure 168. *Working Partners.* Grif Teller.

PERSPECTIVE PROJECTION

There are three kinds of perspective views:
one-point, two-point, and three-point. The
numbers refer to the number of vanishing
points generated by each view. The orientation of the viewed object relative to the
picture plane determines how many vanishing points are generated.

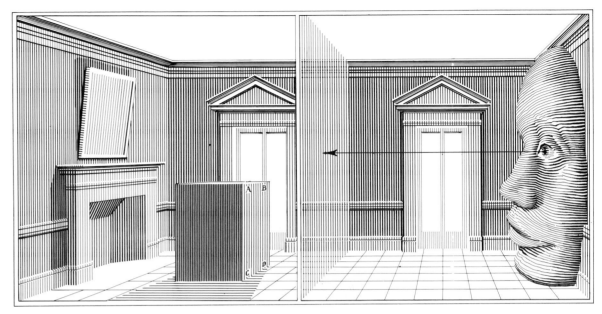

One-point perspective   Two of an object's
spatial axes are parallel to the picture plane.
One vanishing point is generated by the one
axis that is not parallel to the picture plane.
Figure 169.

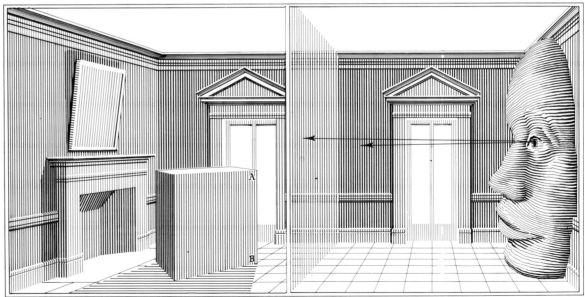

Two-point perspective   One of an object's
spatial axes is parallel to the picture plane.
Two vanishing points are generated by the
two axes that are not parallel to the picture
plane.   Figure 170.

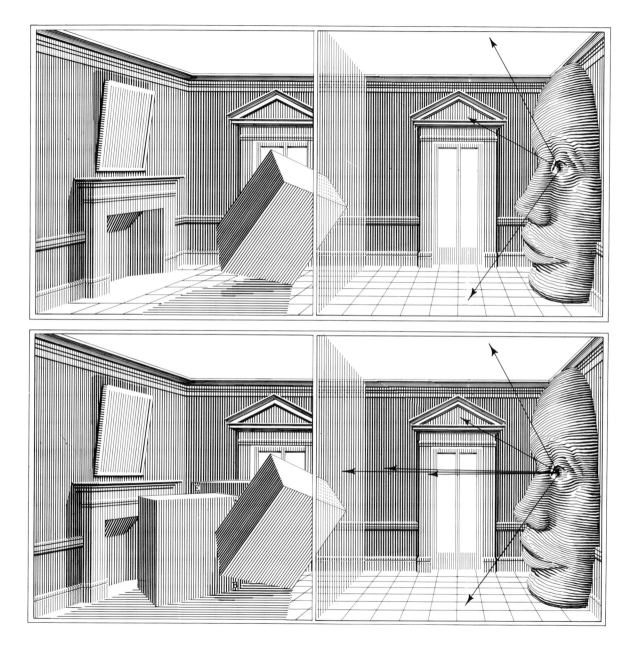

Three-point perspective None of the object's three spatial axes is parallel to the picture plane. Three vanishing points are generated by the three axes that are not parallel to the picture plane. Figure 171.

Combined perspective When several objects of different orientation are present, then the number of vanishing points generated is the sum of all the vanishing points generated by the individual objects. Figure 172.

PERSPECTIVE PROJECTION

Office Method

Perspective views of the office method are constructed from the combined information of two or more orthographic views. A plan contributes horizontal information. Another view, either a section or elevation, contributes vertical information.

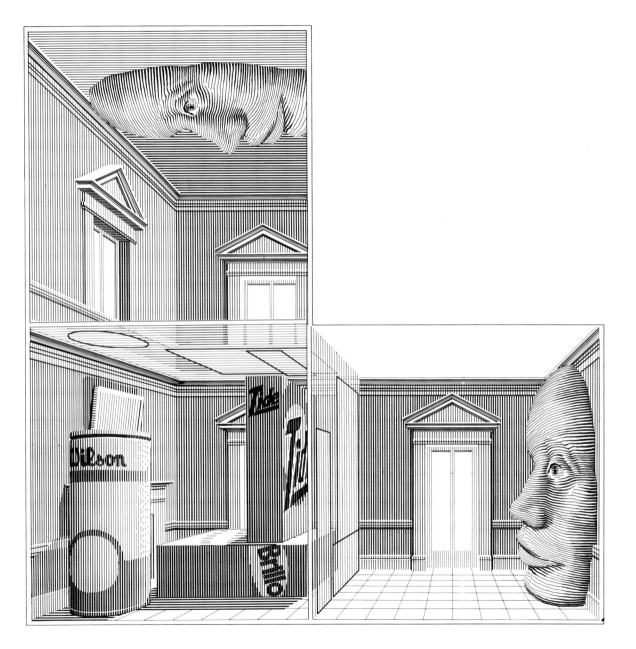

Figure 173. *The Office Method.* At least two orthographic views are required for an office method view.

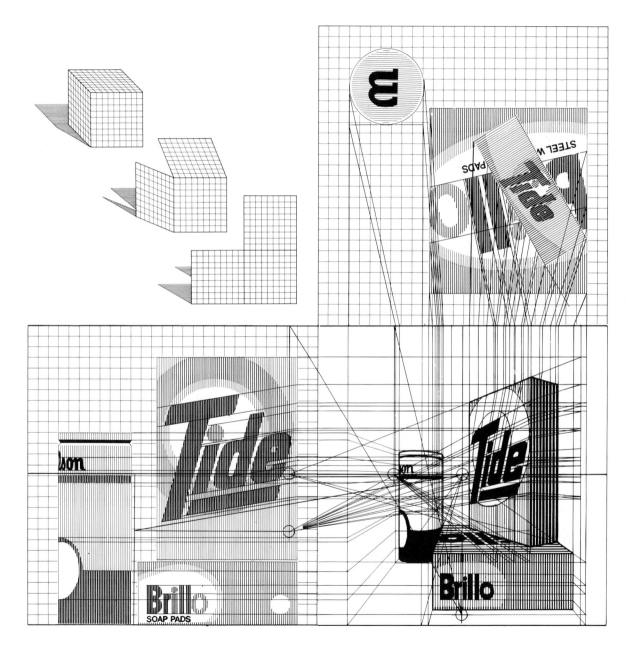

The information of the two views is combined to form the perspective by first rotating the several views until they lie in the same plane.

Figure 174. *The Office Method.* The information of the two views is combined to form the perspective.

159

PERSPECTIVE PROJECTION

Office Method:
A Glossary of Terms

Before proceeding with an explanation of how to construct a perspective by using the office method, it is important to define some of the terms that will be used along the way.

Center of vision (CV) The point on the picture plane at which the viewer is looking.

Picture plane (PP) A plane analogous to a window through which drawings are projected. Figure 175.

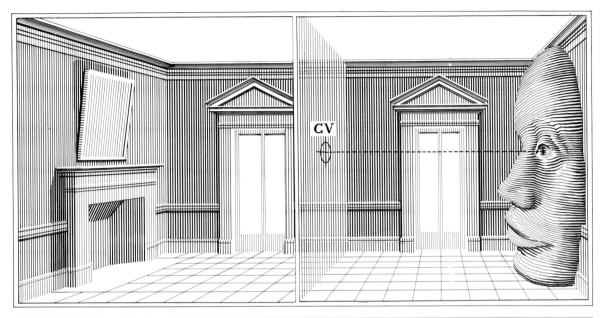

Cone of vision In perspective projection, a conical field of vision radiating outward from the viewer along the viewer's line of sight. In perspective practice, cones of vision are used to define breadths of field within which only acceptable levels of distortion can be expected to occur. Commonly, an acceptable cone of vision is taken as 60° (30° radiating about the line of sight). Figure 176.

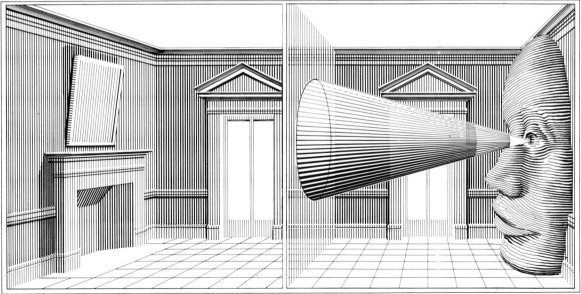

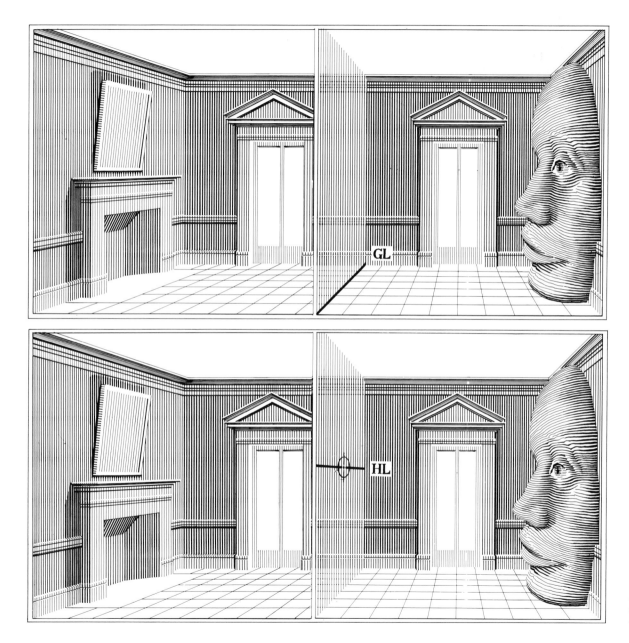

Ground line (GL) In perspective projection, a line on the picture plane where the ground or assumed ground intersects the picture plane. Figure 177.

Horizon line (HL) In perspective projection, a line on the picture plane that is parallel to the ground and passes through the center of vision (that point on the picture plane at which the viewer is looking). The horizon line is always drawn at the height of the viewer's eyes. Vanishing points of lines parallel to the ground are located along the horizon line. Figure 178.

PERSPECTIVE PROJECTION

Office Method:
A Glossary of Terms

Vertical measuring line (VML) In perspective projection, a line on the picture plane where vertical information can be drawn to scale. Where a plane already intersects the picture plane, height can be measured along its line of intersection with the picture plane; where a plane does not already intersect the picture plane, height can be measured by first extending that plane up to or back to a line of intersection with the picture plane and by then measuring along that line of intersection. Figure 179.

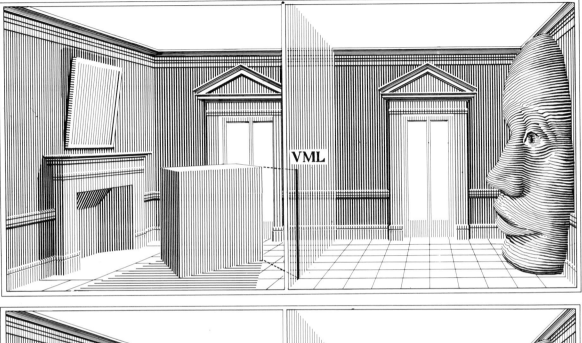

Sight line A line of projection to or through the picture plane. Sight lines determine points on the picture plane that correspond to points on viewed objects. Depending upon the projective system used, sight lines can be oblique (intersecting the picture plane at an angle other than 90°), orthogonal (intersecting the picture plane exclusively at 90°), or convergent (converging to a single point). Figure 180.

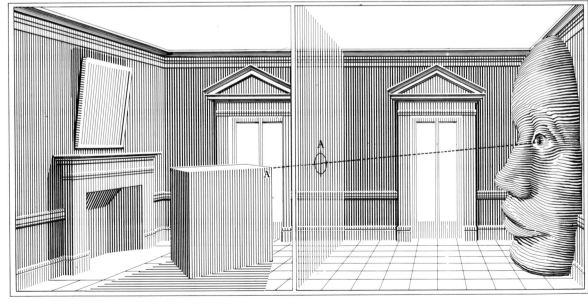

162

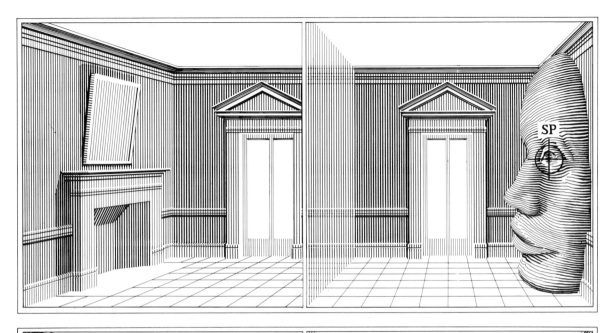

Station point (SP) In perspective projection, the assumed position of the viewer's eye. Figure 181.

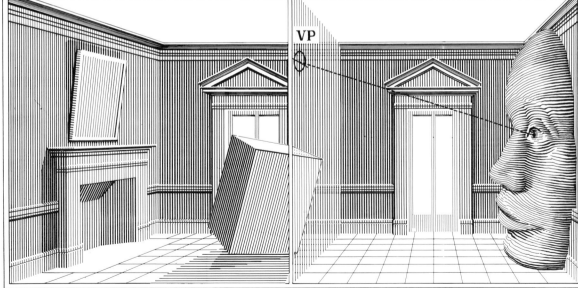

Vanishing point (VP) In perspective projection, a point on the picture plane at which a set of parallel lines appear to converge. The vanishing point for a given set of parallel lines is found by drawing a line parallel to that set from the station point to a point of intersection with the picture plane. That point of intersection with the picture plane is the vanishing point for the set. One rule of thumb is that the vanishing point for any set of lines that is horizontal (parallel to the ground) must occur along the horizon line. Figure 182.

PERSPECTIVE PROJECTION

Office Method

Step 1: locating the station point As has been pointed out earlier, perspective is unique among projective systems in that it yields the view from one individual and singular point in space. It is with the location of that point, which is called the *station point,* that the process begins.

1.1 Determine the desired direction or line of sight from which you will view the building (frontal, lateral, etc.). Then position the plan accordingly with the line of sight represented with a vertical line on your drawing board.

1.2 Decide how much of the building you want to show. Do you want to show the whole building, in which case you would want to stand further away, or do you want to show a detail of the building, in which case you would want to stand closer?

1.3 Locate the station point (SP) along the line of sight. It should be positioned back far enough from the building that what you will want to show (whether detail or whole building from step 2) would fit within a reasonable cone of vision. For most uses a reasonable cone of vision is taken as 60°. In the example at right a cone of vision of 30° has been used.

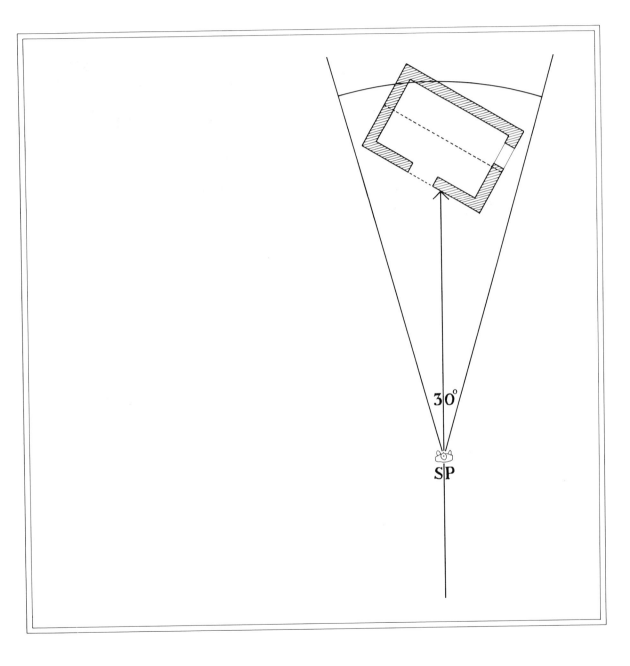

Figure 183. *Office Method Step 1.*

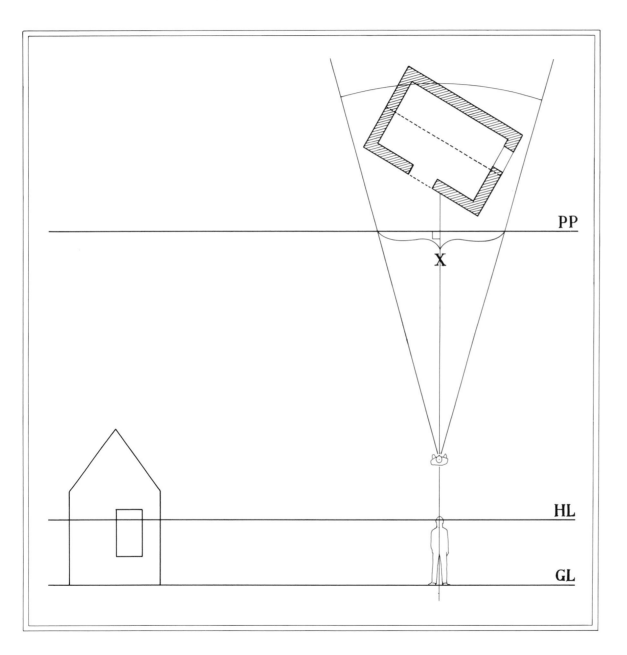

PP

X

HL

GL

Step 2: locating the picture plane It is through the use of a picture plane, which may be considered as analogous to a window or a projection screen in a cinema, that a perspective is constructed. The picture plane is located as follows:

2.1 Decide the size of the view. This decision might be based upon: 1) the size of available paper, 2) the medium to be used and its implications as to size, 3) the level of detail desirable in the view, and 4) the distances from which the drawing is to be viewed.

2.2 In plan, position the picture plane (PP) such that, given your decisions in steps 1.2 and 2.1, that picture plane will intercept your cone of vision at a width x equal to your desired width for the view. The picture plane must be perpendicular to the line of sight.

2.3 Square to the line of sight and to the left (or right) of the area where you will draw the perspective, position an elevation or section of the building. Then, at appropriate heights relative to that elevation, draw horizontals representing the ground line (GL) and the horizon line (HL). The horizon line represents the height of the viewer's eye. It is drawn to scale at that distance from the ground line at which the viewer's eye is located relative to the ground.

Figure 184. *Office Method Step 2.*

PERSPECTIVE PROJECTION

Office Method

Step 3: locating vanishing points It is through the use of vanishing points that perspectives achieve their sense of depth. Vanishing points for horizontal lines, of which the instance at right can be expected to yield two, are located as follows.

3.1 In plan, draw lines parallel to the sets of lines (side A and side B) for which you want to find vanishing points. These lines should be drawn from the station point (SP) out to points of intersection with the picture plane (PP).

3.2 Project these points of intersection with the picture plane (PP) to equivalent positions on the horizon line (HL). These resultant points are the vanishing points for the two sides of the building, vanishing point left (VPL) for side A and vanishing point right (VPR) for side B.

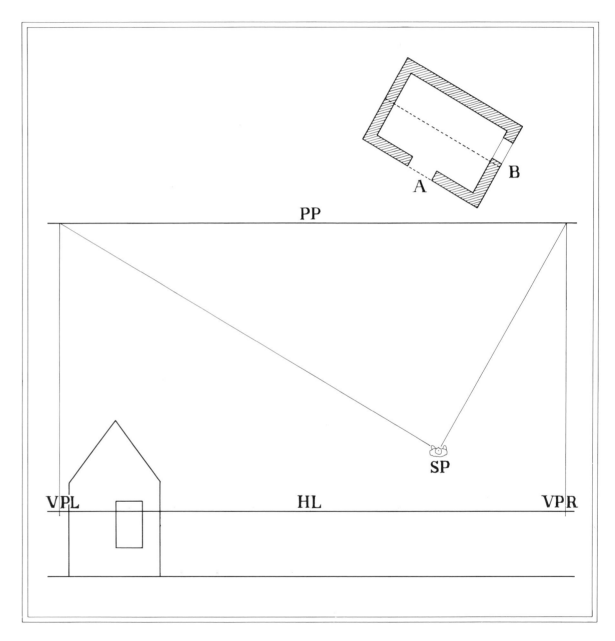

Figure 185. *Office Method Step 3.*

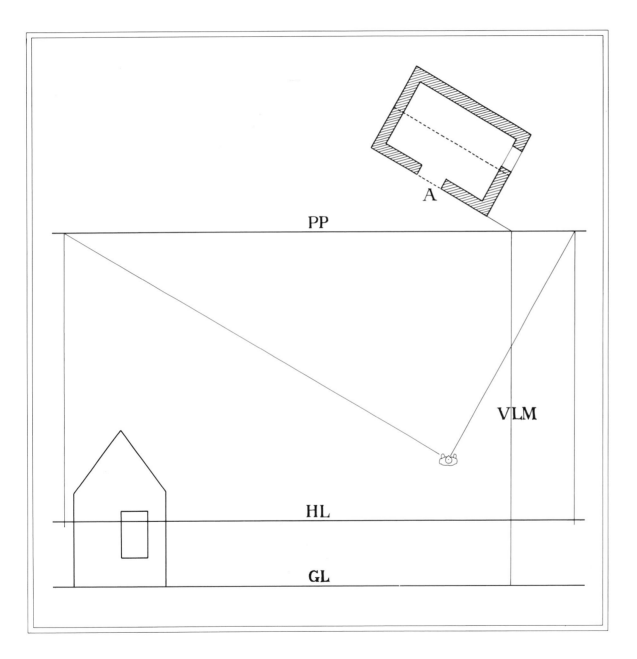

PP

VLM

HL

GL

A

Step 4: vertical line of measure While perspectives are not scaled drawings in the sense that they can be used to encode dimensions, they are still drawn in reference to the true sizes of things. Information about the true sizes of things is entered into the process of perspective construction through the use of what is called the vertical line of measure. A vertical line of measure can be constructed only on the picture plane, but it serves as a source of measure for all dimensions of height, whether they are in front of the picture plane or behind the picture plane. It is located for any appropriate side (in the example to the left side A is used) of the building as follows:

4.1 In plan, extend side A to a point of intersection with the picture plane (PP). If side A already intersects the picture plane, you can proceed directly to step 4.2.

4.2 Project that point of intersection vertically down the drawing until it crosses both the horizon line (HL) and the ground line (GL). This vertical line is the vertical line of measure (VLM). If side A had already intersected the picture plane, you would have merely projected the VLM from that point of intersection.

Figure 186. *Office Method Step 4.*

167

PERSPECTIVE PROJECTION

Office Method

Step 5: entering vertical information Vertical information is commonly entered through the use of a section or an elevation such as the one already positioned in the instance at right. The process is one merely of projecting that information at scale to the vertical line of measure (VLM).

5.1 From relevant points on the elevation of side A or side B, project horizontals to points of intersection with the vertical line of measure (VLM).

5.2 From these points of intersection, vanish this relevant vertical information to the vanishing point of side A (VPL).

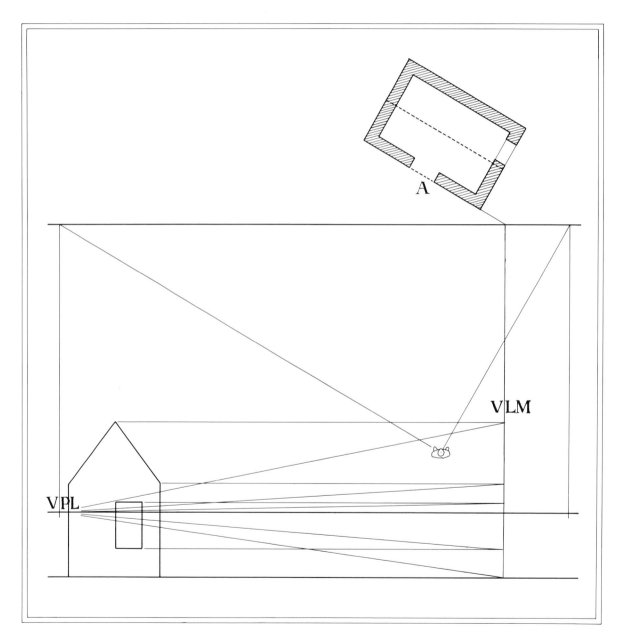

Figure 187. *Office Method Step 5.*

168

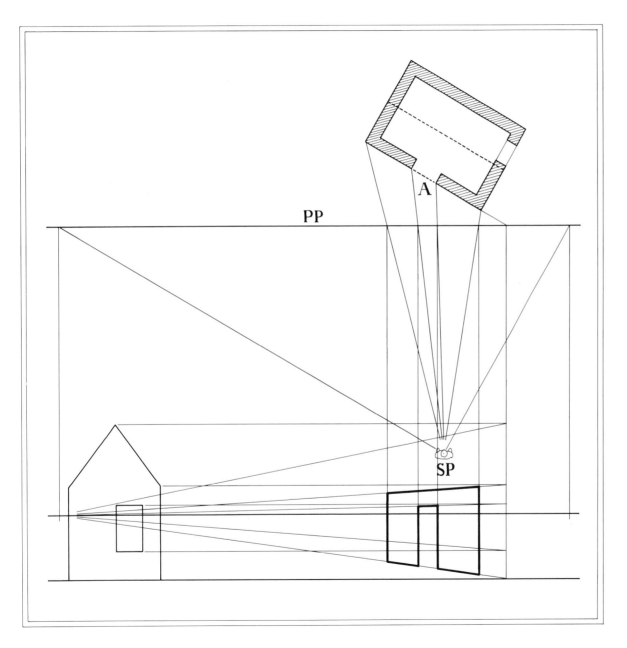

PP

A

SP

Step 6: constructing one face You now have sufficient vertical information to proceed with the perspective of the building. This is accomplished by first generating a representation of one face of the building and then using this one part to generate the perspective of the whole. In the instance at left, side A is used for this purpose. Given that the vertical information for side A is already present in the lines vanished to VPL (step 5.2), you can proceed to generating the lateral information for side A, which is done in plan through a process called *sighting*.

6.1 In plan, sight relevant points along side A to points of intersection with the picture plane by drawing sight lines back through the picture plane that converge at the station point (SP). Project these points of intersection on the picture plane vertically along lines that cross the lines converging at VPL.

6.2 You can now proceed to draw side A in perspective. Use the points of intersection of the projected vertical information, the lines converging at VPL, together with the lateral information of side A brought down from the picture plane.

Figure 188. *Office Method Step 6.*

PERSPECTIVE PROJECTION

Office Method

Step 7: completing the perspective From the roof peak base and edges of side A, vanish lines to VPR.

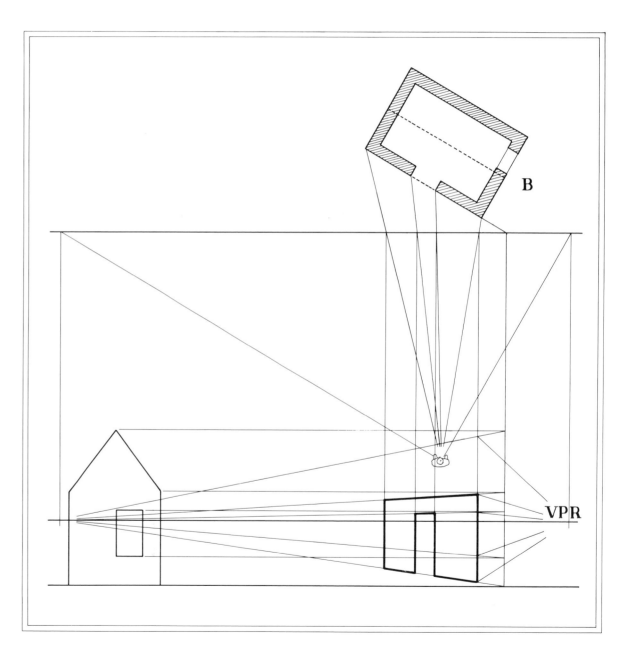

Figure 189. *Office Method Step 7.*

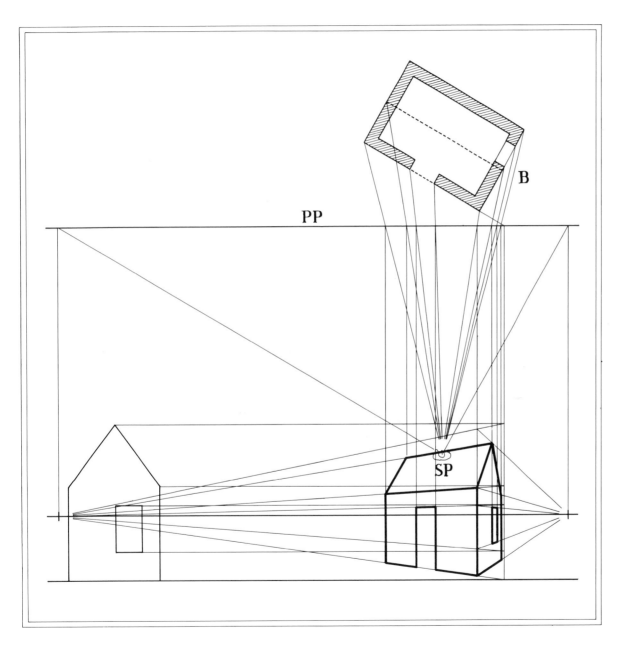

Step 8: completing the perspective Construct side B. In plan, sight relevant points along side B to points of intersection with the picture plane by drawing sight lines back through the picture plane that converge at the station point (SP). Project these points of intersection on the picture plane vertically along lines that cross the lines from the roof peak, eave, and base converging at VPR.

B

PP

SP

Figure 190. *Office Method Step 8.*

171

PERSPECTIVE PROJECTION

One-point Magic Method

Using a one-point construction called the *magic method,* we can dispense altogether with the process of sighting on plans and determine foreshortening by projecting distance points on a section or elevation. This method is based on Alberti's system from the mid-fifteenth century, which had concluded a long search for an accurate method of foreshortening.[11]

Like Alberti's, the *magic method* is based on the fact that the vanishing point of a 45° spatial diagonal must be the same distance (at left or at right of the central vanishing point) as the viewer is standing from the picture plane. Most importantly, this point (VP 45°) can be found without using a station point or projecting lines to the picture plane. Rather, it can be laid out directly on the picture plane (for which an existing section or elevation is conveniently used) merely by measuring over to the left or right of the central vanishing point the assumed distance of the viewer from the picture plane. Since they are constructed quickly from orthographic views, *magic* views are used to rapidly test design proposals at an early point. As indicated,

---

[11] Alberti's system was the basis of the *pavimenti,* a system of drawing floor tiles, that was used by the early Renaissance perspectivists. For a thorough account of Alberti's method consult: L. Wright, *Perspective in Perspective* (London: Routledge & Kegan Paul, 1983) pp. 64-81.

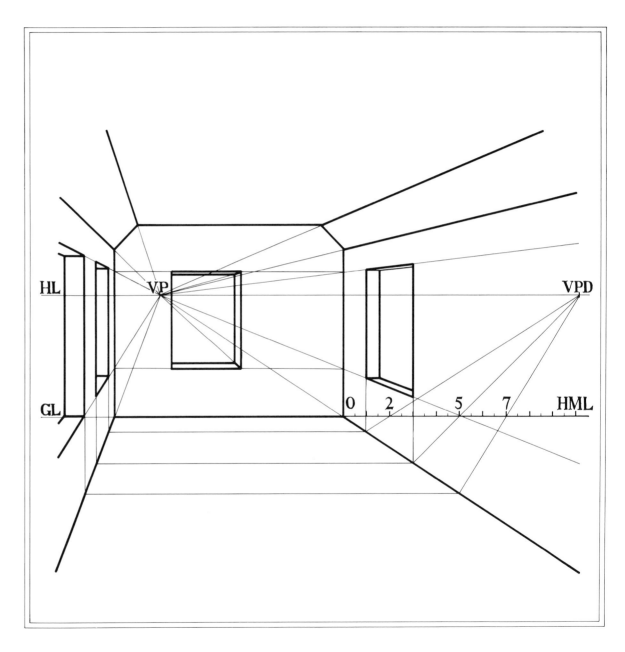

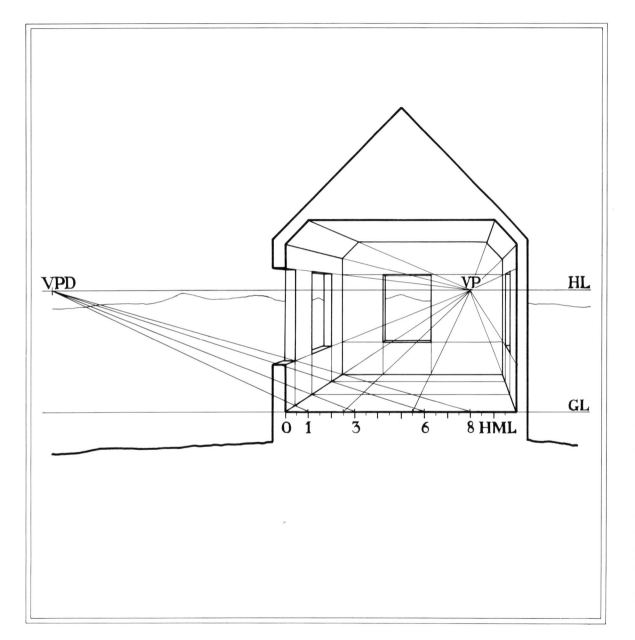

there are two types, one using an end wall elevation, and the other a cross-section. The former develops the view out from the assumed picture plane and the latter behind it.

Interior from elevation 1) Draw ground and horizon lines (GL, HL). 2) Locate central vanishing point (CV). 3) Locate vanishing point for diagonal (VPD) left or right of central vanishing point. 4) Use CV to vanish edges of floor and ceiling out from the elevation. 5) Construct a horizontal measuring line (HML) located along the ground line so that zero (no depth from the elevation) is at the lower left or right outside corner of the elevation. 6) Use HML together with VPD to project increments of depth to the right or left edge of the floor, and project these points out into the interior of the room.[12] Figure 191.

Interior from section 1) Draw ground and horizon lines (GL, HL). 2) Locate the central vanishing point (CV). 3) Locate the vanishing point for the diagonal (VPD) left or right of the central vanishing point. 4) Vanish edges of ceilings, floors and walls from the section back toward the CV. 5) Construct a horizontal measuring line (HML). HML should be located along the ground line so that zero is at the lower left or right inside corner of the section. Use HML together with VPD to project increments of depth to the right or left edge of floor. Project these points out into the room.[13] Figure 192.

[12] Kevin Forseth, *Graphics for Architecture* (New York: Van Nostrand Reinhold Co., 1980) p. 142.

[13] Kevin Forseth, *Graphics for Architecture* p. 140.

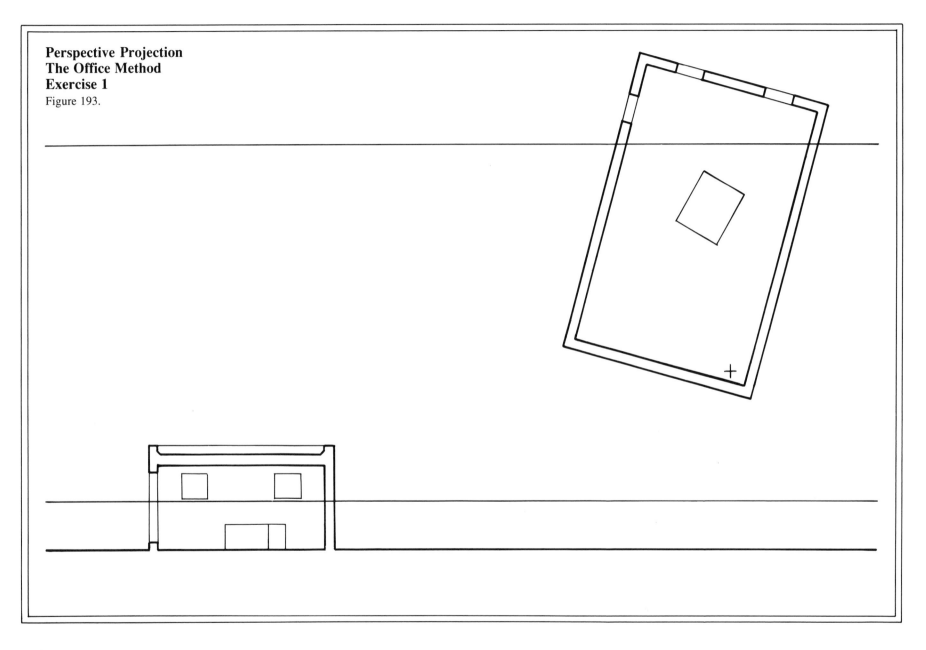

Perspective Projection
The Office Method
Exercise 1
Figure 193.

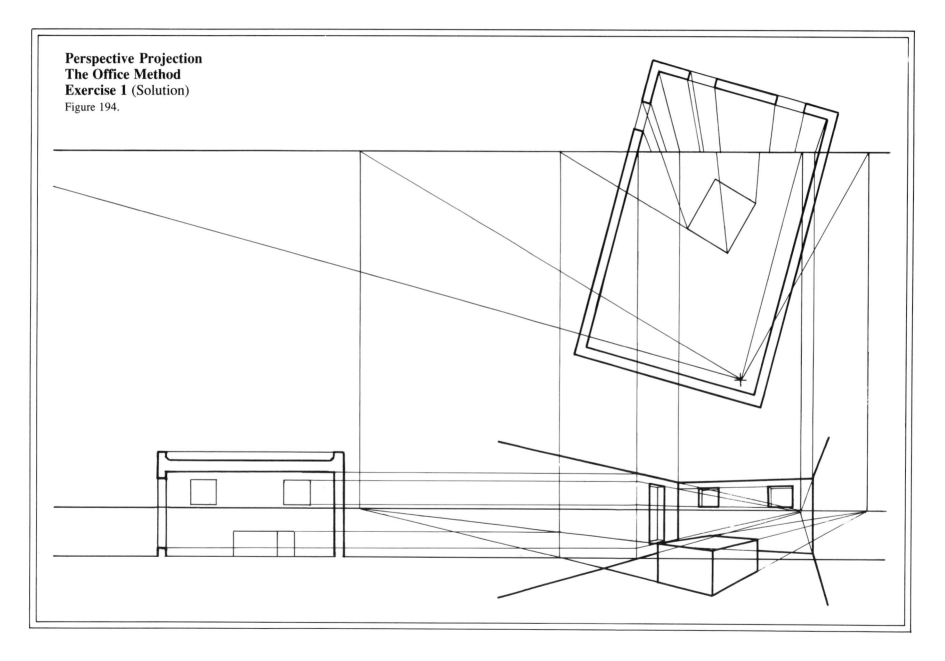

**Perspective Projection
The Office Method
Exercise 1** (Solution)
Figure 194.

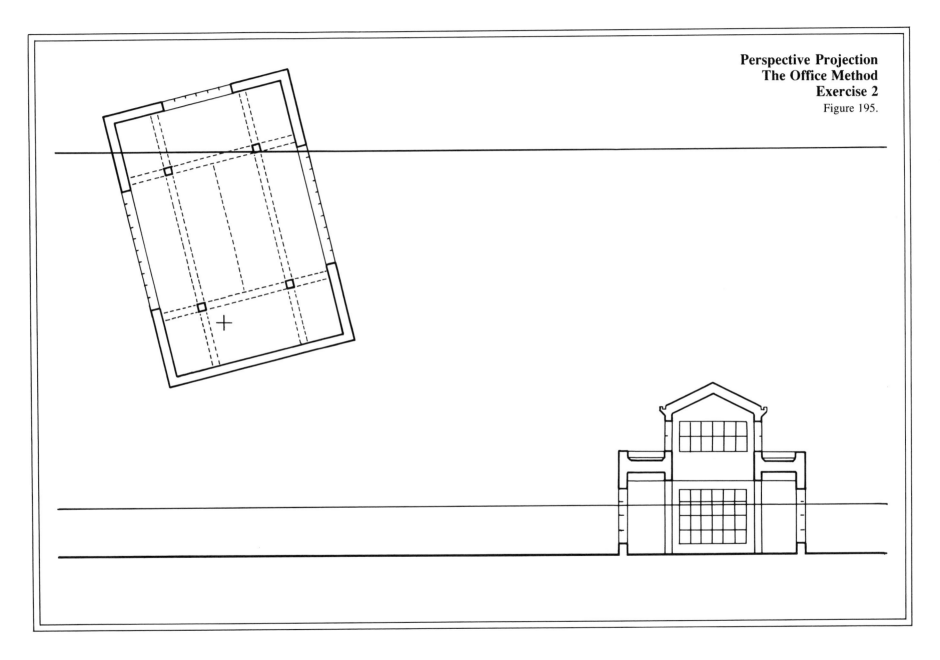

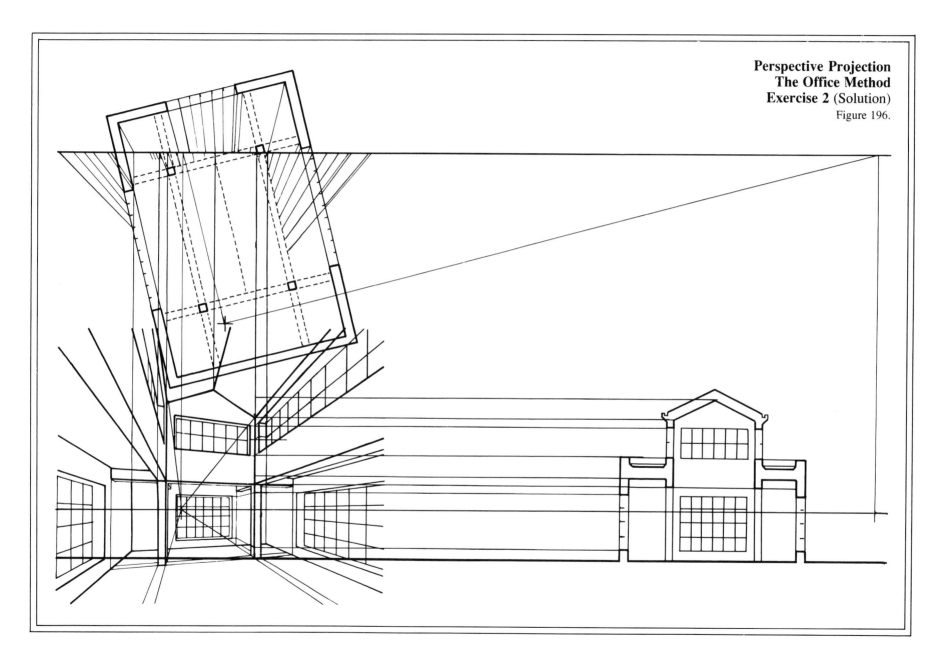

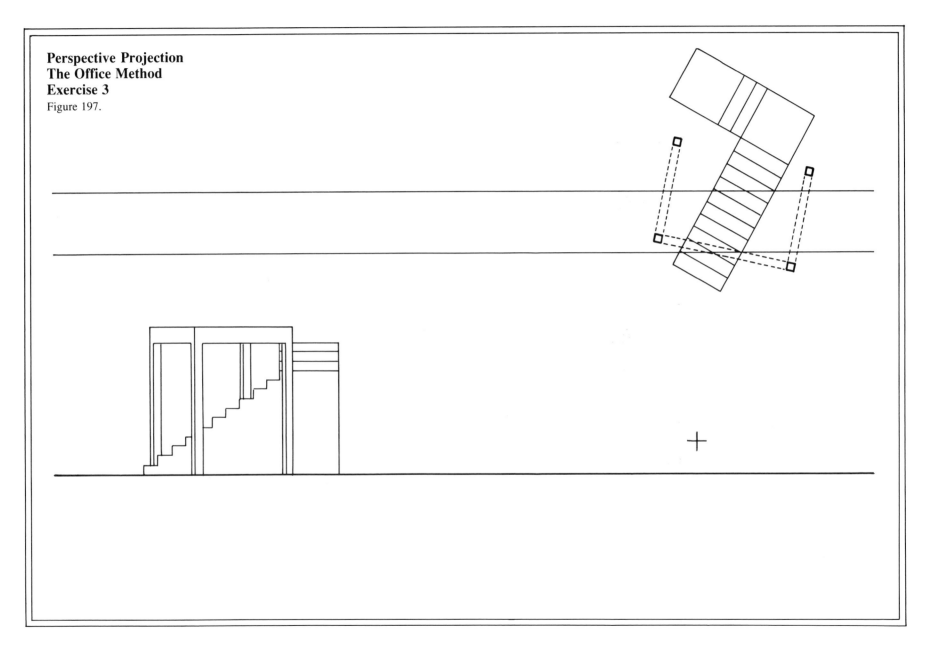

Perspective Projection
The Office Method
Exercise 3

Figure 197.

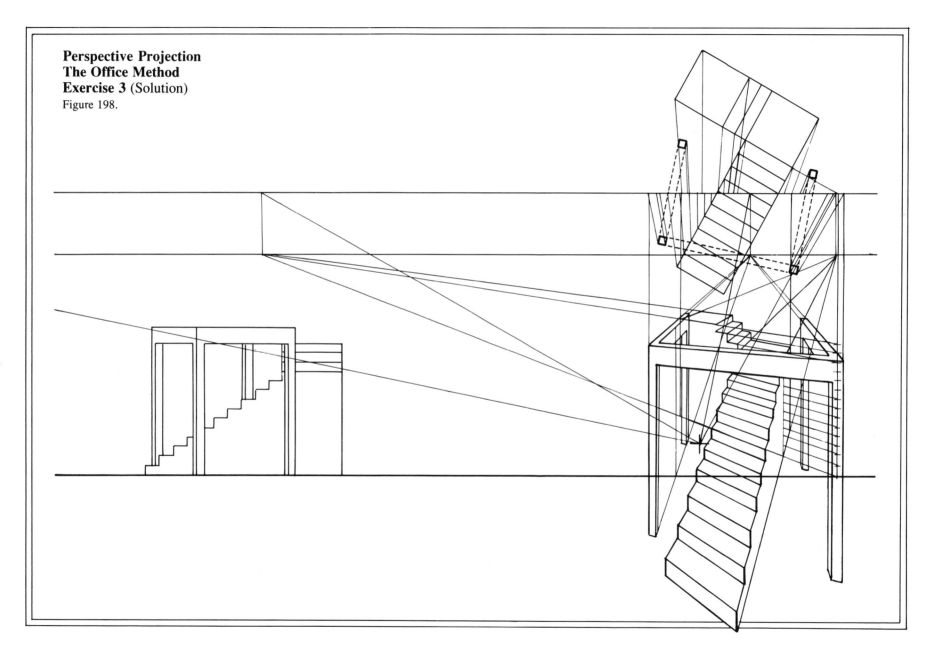

Perspective Projection
The Office Method
Exercise 3 (Solution)
Figure 198.

PERSPECTIVE PROJECTION
Project 1
Extended Perspective from Plan and Section

This project calls for generating a large (at least 24 inches wide) freehand constructed perspective view. Begin by selecting a large public hall or industrial facility that is characterized by a well-articulated structural bay. Using on-site estimates, generate scaled plans and sections (the latter must show an interior elevation).

In a straight-edge drawing, generate a spatial armature for the space. This should recognize the size of the ultimate view and follow the process outlined in the previous pages describing the *office method:* 1) select your station point, 2) locate your picture plane, 3) locate vanishing points, 4) generate a vertical line of measure, and so on. This drawing should be carefully executed but lightly drawn as an underlay for the freehand drawing that is to follow.

When the drawing of the armature has been completed, in a strong, freehand line, generate a full perspective representation of the space. This drawing should be carried through to a highly resolved level of detail.

Materials: Pencils, 2H (for straight-line construction), 4B (for freehand), transparent trace.

Figure 199. David Celento.
Figure 200. (opposite page) detail, David Celento.

180

PERSPECTIVE PROJECTION
Project 2
Making Perspective Move

In the extended discussion of Kent Bloomer's assignment in chapter 3, it was stated that his requirement that we show two places—outside and inside—at once had freed us from the grip of perspective. So long as they require changing the direction of view, even optical assignments can make a similar contribution. Consistent with the sense of precision of this more optically directed chapter, the following aims to further knowledge of perspective construction and knowledge of its limitations.

The project Find a condition that defies complete description by a single-view perspective. It should be a scene that seems to have several points of focus, several directions in which you are tempted to look. Then using several central vanishing points, generate a view that documents and resolves the changing optical array as you move your direction of gaze. Your view should generate at least two central vanishing points. As examples, the view immediately to the right has seven and the view on the opposite page has four.

Figure 201. *Galleria Vittorio Emanuele*. Douglas Cooper, 1976, carbon pencil on paper, 96" x 96" (private collection) Photo: Wolfgang Sprang.

Figure 202. *Die Kneipe*. Douglas Cooper, 1984, carbon pencil on paper, 96" x 144" (private collection) Photo: David Aschkenas.

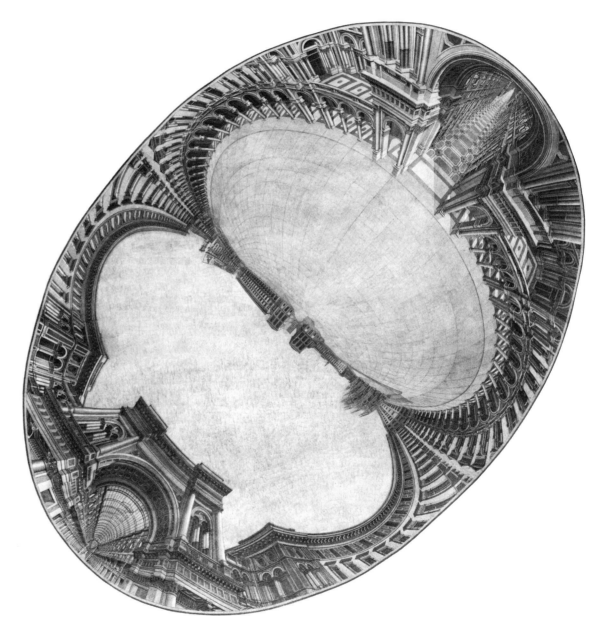

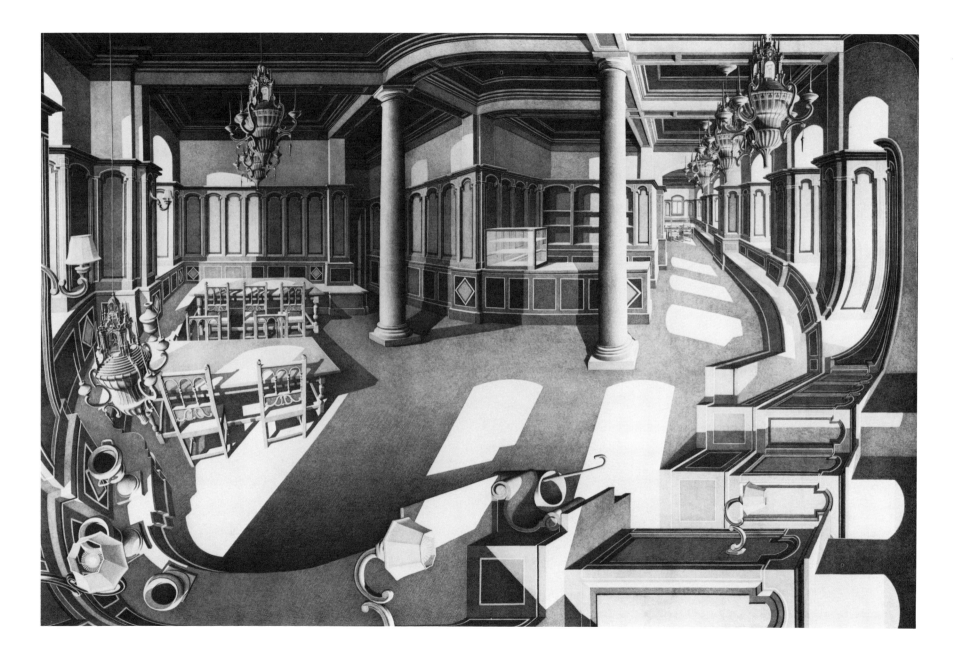

PERSPECTIVE PROJECTION
Project 3
Making Perspectives Like Orthographic Views and Vice Versa.

Differences among orthographic, paraline, and perspective views have been elaborated at length. Within this discussion, it is easy to forget what is common to them all, that they offer views of the visual world. As a consequence, we can feel somewhat at the mercy of convention. This project aims at restoring some sense of ease about projective systems in general, as well as some sense of using them to serve our intentions independently of conventional usage. The project calls for combining the three into one expression.

The project Find a condition that supports both orthographic and perspective description. The circumstance should have some parts that are predominated by a sense of frontality or plan; at the same time, it should have other conditions where perspective seems predominant. Then in one view describe the entire condition in a way that allows each part to be shown as it is best shown. Strong plan elements should be shown in plan. Strong elevational elements should be shown in elevation (or oblique). Strong directional views should be shown in perspective. At the same time, seek to resolve each of the separate characteristic views with each other so that a unified whole results.

As examples, the view at right shows the facade frontally, the floor of the nave in plan,

the cupola in plan, and the square in front, the interior of the nave, and the outside of the church in perspective. Likewise, the view opposite shows the powerhouse and bridges in paraline, the baseball park in plan, and the view up the street at right and the buildings on the top of the hill in perspective.

Figure 203. *S. Christoforis, Siena.* Douglas Cooper, 1971, 8" x 10" (from the author's sketchbook) Photo: David Aschkenas.

Figure 204. (opposite page) *Panther Hallow.* Douglas Cooper, 1989, charcoal on paper, 56" x 80" (detail only) Photo: David Aschkenas.

184

185

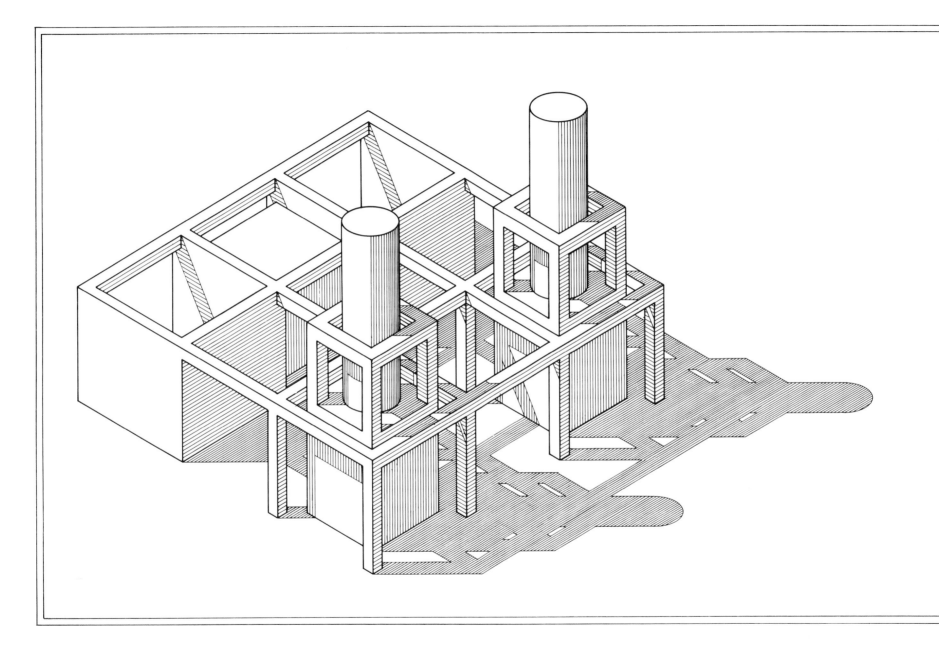

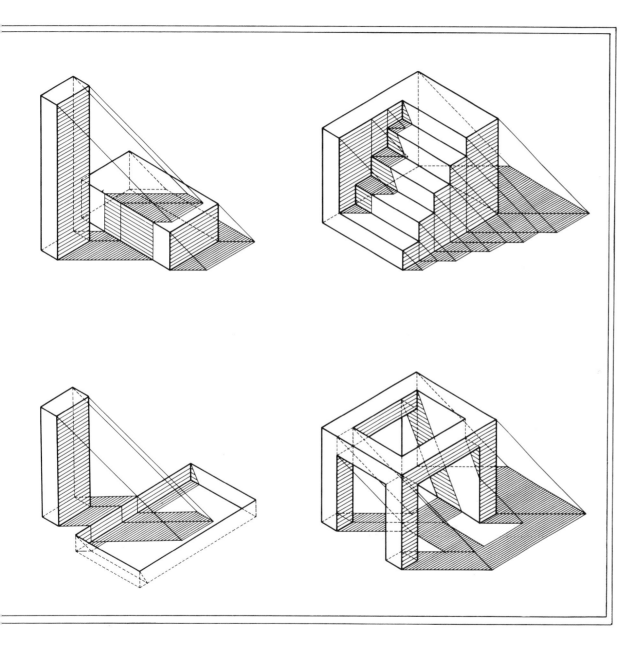

SHADE AND SHADOW
IN ISOMETRIC PROJECTION [14]

This volume concludes with the study of shade and shadow casting in isometric projection and, in the next section, in orthographic projection. Shadow casting always used to be included within courses in projective geometry as one of its more accessible areas of study. However, with the arrival of the computer, and a consequent reduction of the need for shadow casting within practice, it is taught less and less frequently to students of architecture and design. This trend is sad, for shadow casting was never just a tool. The significance of shadow casting within any drawing curriculum is its function as a hurdle. It teaches and tests capabilities of three-dimensional visualization that are more far-reaching than any application it may no longer have in practice.

Because its process is easier to visualize in a representation that shows all three spatial axes simultaneously, it is best to begin the subject with isometric projection.

Figure 205. *Shade and Shadow in Isometric Projection.*

[14] Adapted from: Maxwell G. Mayo, *Line and Light* (Pittsburgh: Department of Architecture, Carnegie Mellon University, 1971) Chapters 1-9.

SHADE AND SHADOW IN ISOMETRIC PROJECTION

Three conventions are used to represent the angle of the light used to project shadows in isometric projection. These conventions are largely a matter of their convenience in using the 30°-60°-90° and 45°-45°-90° triangles that are common to offices. Only one, R°, has any significance beyond convenience, that being that it represents the volumetric diagonal of a cube.

R° light R° light is defined as light whose azimuth, measured clockwise from north, is 225°, and whose altitude, measured from the horizontal ground plane, is 35°15'51". R° light is further defined as light that is parallel to the southwest diagonal of a cube oriented normally to the north-south-east-west axes. When represented in isometric projection, as shown at right, R° light is represented by a line drawn at an angle of 30° to the horizontal.

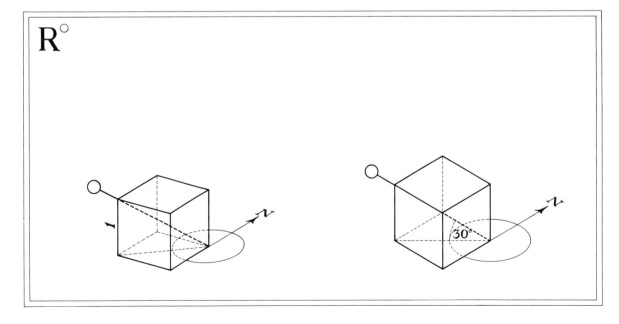

Figure 206. *R° light.*

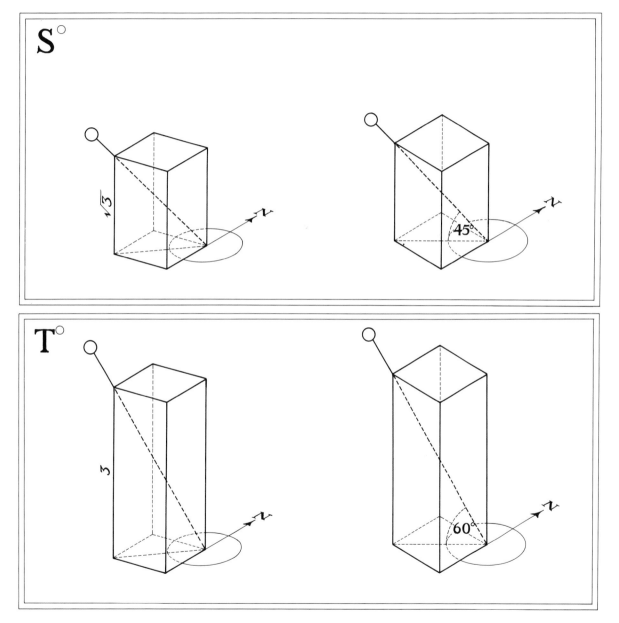

S° light S° light is defined as light whose azimuth, measured clockwise from north is 225°, and whose altitude, measured from the horizontal ground plane, is 50°46'15". S° light is further defined as light that is parallel to the southwest diagonal of a 1 x 1 x 2 rectangular solid oriented normally to the north-south-east-west axes. When represented in isometric projection, as shown at left, S° light is represented by a line drawn at an angle of 45° to the horizontal.

Figure 207. *S° light.*

T° light T° light is defined as light whose azimuth, measured clockwise from north is 225°, and whose altitude, measured from the horizontal ground line, is 65°45'36". T° light is further defined as light that is parallel to the southwest diagonal of a 1 x1 x 3 rectangular solid oriented normally to the north-south-east-west axes. When represented in isometric projection, as shown at left, T° light is represented by a line drawn at an angle of 60° to the horizontal.

Figure 208. *T° light.*

189

SHADE AND SHADOW IN
ISOMETRIC PROJECTION

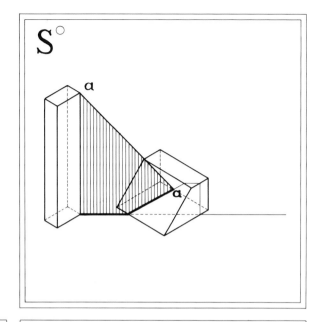

Casting the shadow of a point, the slicing method To cast the shadow of a point, a vertical plane is passed through the object and ground receiving the shadow. This vertical plane lies in the direction of the sun's rays. Where it intersects the object and the ground, is called the *slice*. The shadow of the point must lie somewhere along this line. A ray of the sun is passed through the point and extended until it intersects the slice. This point of intersection between ray and slice is the shadow of the point.

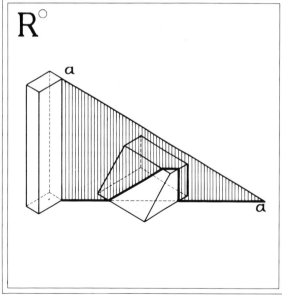

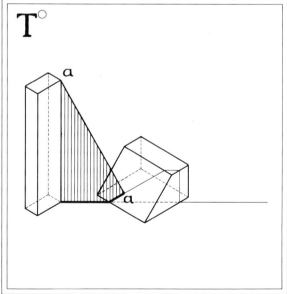

Figure 209. *Casting the shadow of a point.*

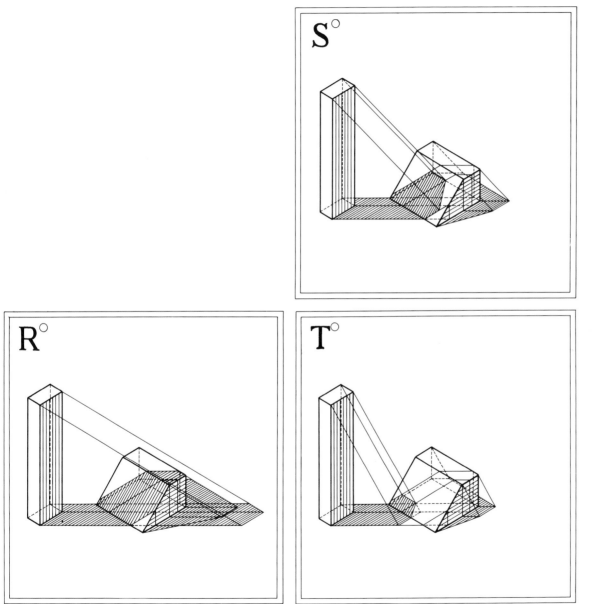

Casting the shadow of a solid To cast the shadow of a solid, the shadows of the solid's vertices are found via the slicing method and then connected.

Figure 210. *Casting the shadow of a solid.*

191

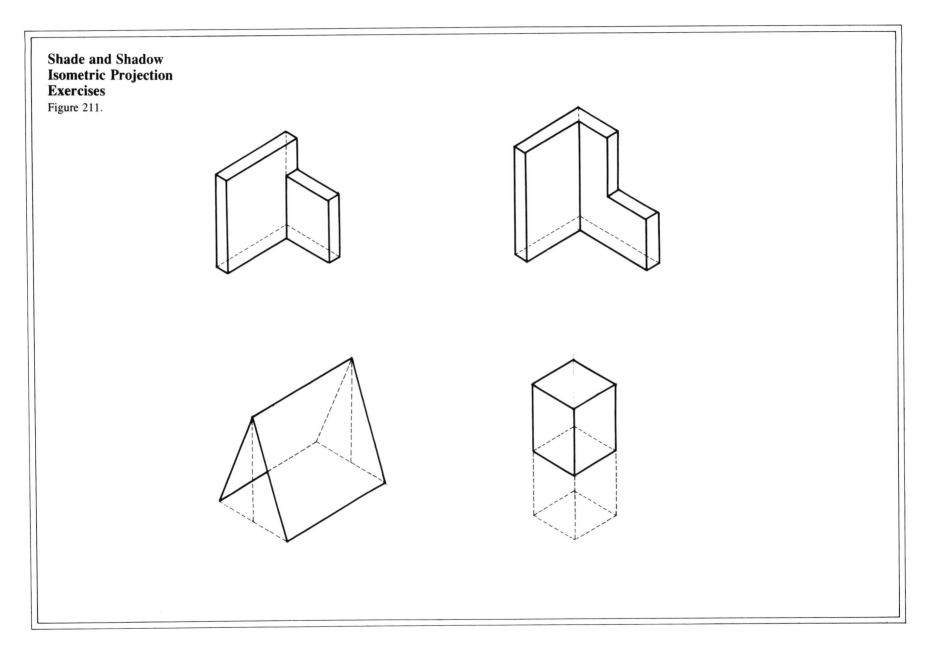

192

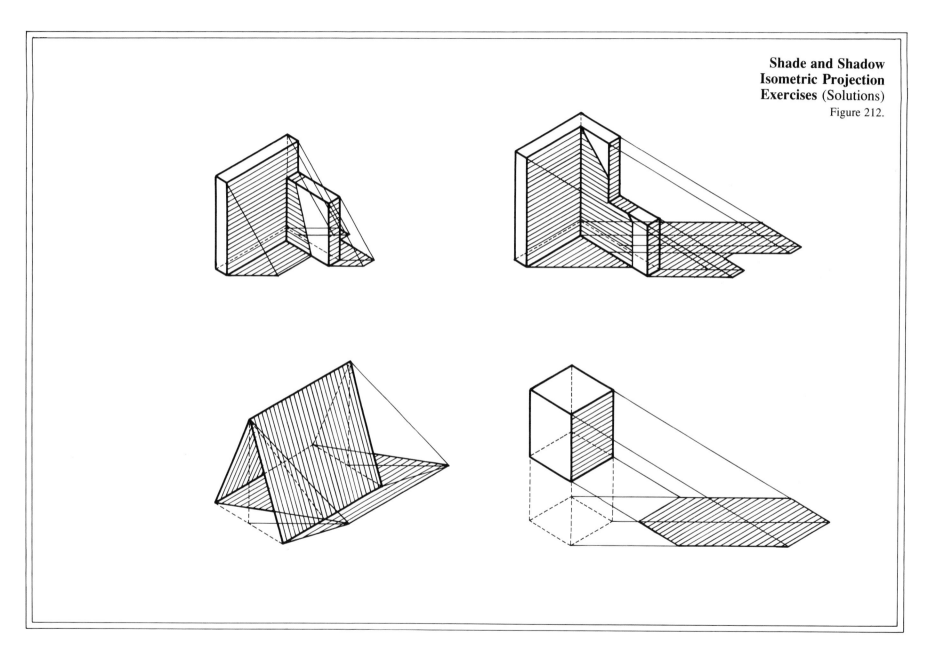

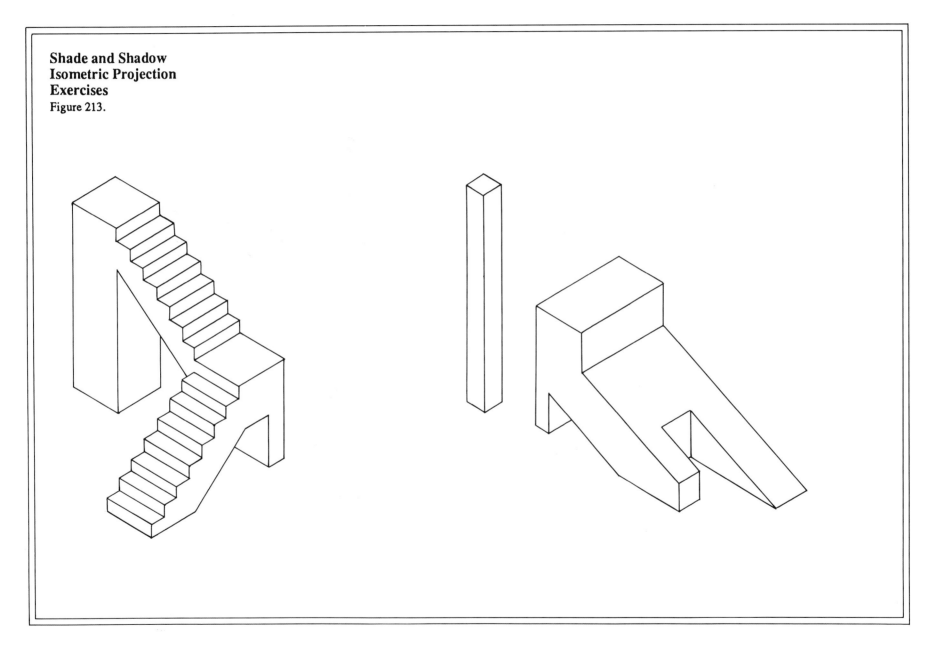

Shade and Shadow
Isometric Projection
Exercises
Figure 213.

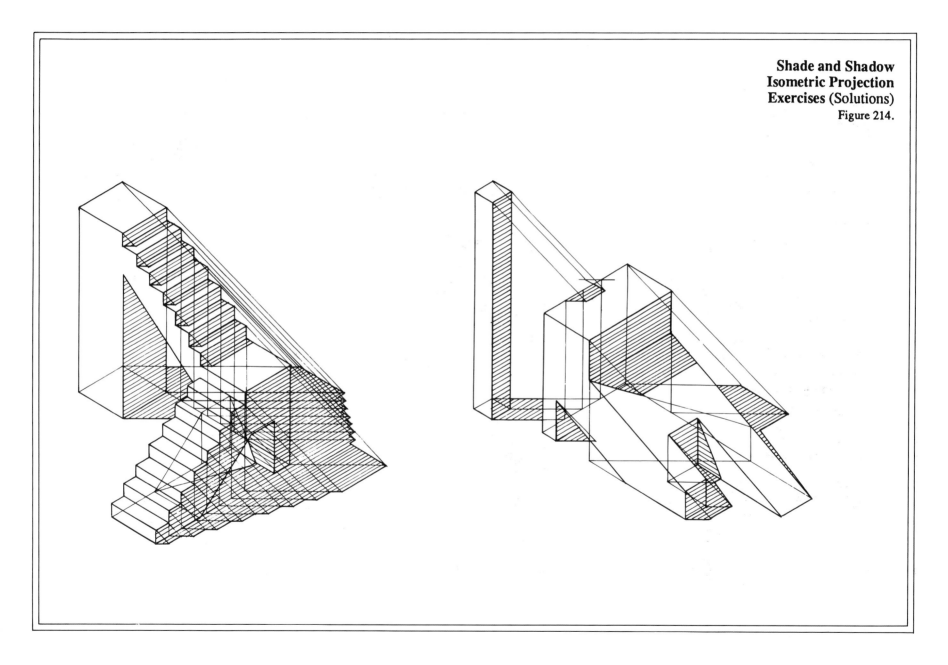

196

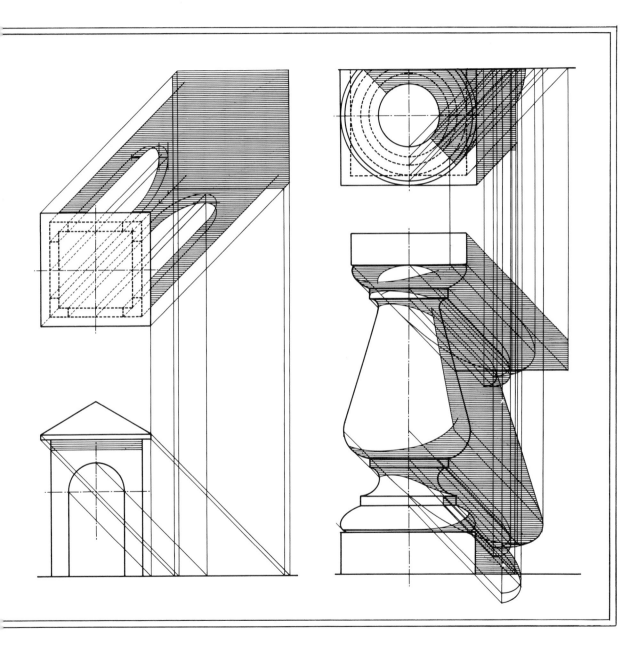

SHADE AND SHADOW IN ORTHOGRAPHIC PROJECTION [15]

Fundamentally, the process of casting shade and shadow in orthographic projection is the same as it is in isometric projection. The slice line is again used. Likewise, we continue to generate shadows point by point and find the shadow of each point at the intersection of the slice line with the ray.

The difference exists only in the fact that the process is conducted over a set of drawings, usually a plan and an elevation, and the work in any one view refers regularly to constructions in the other. Even in this there is a regular pattern. It almost always happens that we begin work in the plan, proceed to the elevation, and then conclude work in the elevation.

Figure 215. *Shade and Shadow in Orthographic Projection.*

[15] Adapted from: Maxwell G. Mayo, *Line and Light* Chapters 1-9.

SHADE AND SHADOW IN ORTHOGRAPHIC PROJECTION

There is one convention governing the direction of light in orthographic projection.

R° light R° light is standard in orthographic projection. R° light has an azimuth of 225° from north and an altitude of 35°15'51". When drawn in plan with north oriented vertically, R° light is represented by a line slanting at 45° toward the upper right. When drawn in east and south elevations, R° light is represented by a line slanting at 45° toward the lower right.

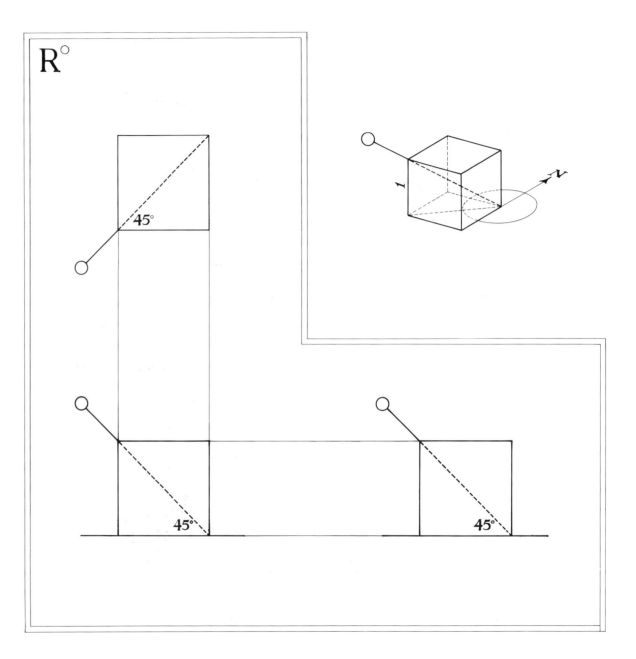

Figure 216. *R° light in orthographic projection*

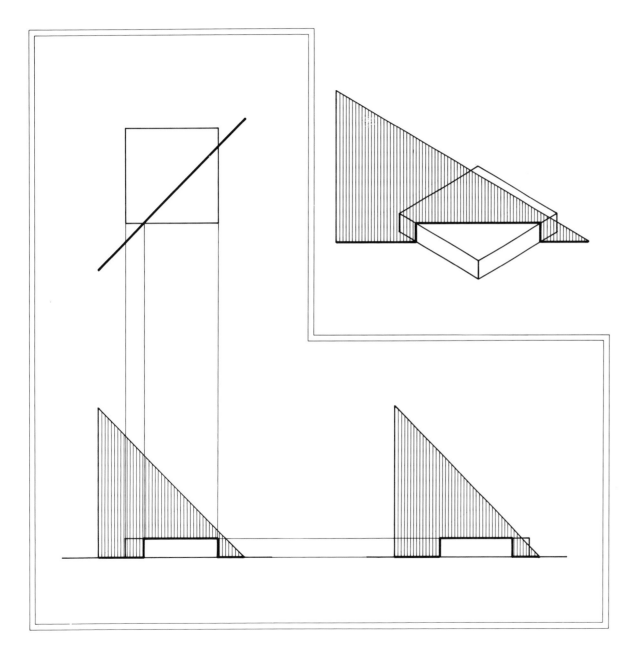

The slicing method Although the process of casting shadows in orthographic projection is essentially the same as it is in isometric projection, the two differ somewhat in technique. While both use the slicing method, the process in orthographic projection requires using a minimum of two drawings (usually a plan and an elevation) and transferring information from one drawing to another. As part of this two-drawing process, the slice is represented in both plan and elevation. Several rules of thumb: 1) In plan, the slice is always represented by a straight line. 2) In elevation, the slice is always represented by a plane.

Figure 217. *The slicing method in orthographic projection.*

SHADE AND SHADOW IN
ORTHOGRAPHIC PROJECTION

Casting the shadow of a point In casting the shadow of a point in orthographic projection, a vertical plane is passed through the point and the object receiving the shadow. The intersection of this plane, the slice, is first drawn in plan. It is always a straight line at 45°. The representation, in plan, of the shadow of the point must lie somewhere along this plan of the slice. Next, through a process of transferring relevant points from the plan of the slice to corresponding points on the objects in the elevation, an elevation of the slice is developed. The position, in elevation, of the shadow of the point must lie somewhere along this elevation of the slice. Then, in elevation, a ray of sunlight is passed through the point and extended to a point of intersection with the elevation of the slice. This point of intersection is the shadow of the point in elevation. Finally, the location of this point is projected from the elevation to a point of intersection with the plan of the slice in the plan view. This point of intersection is the shadow of the point in plan.

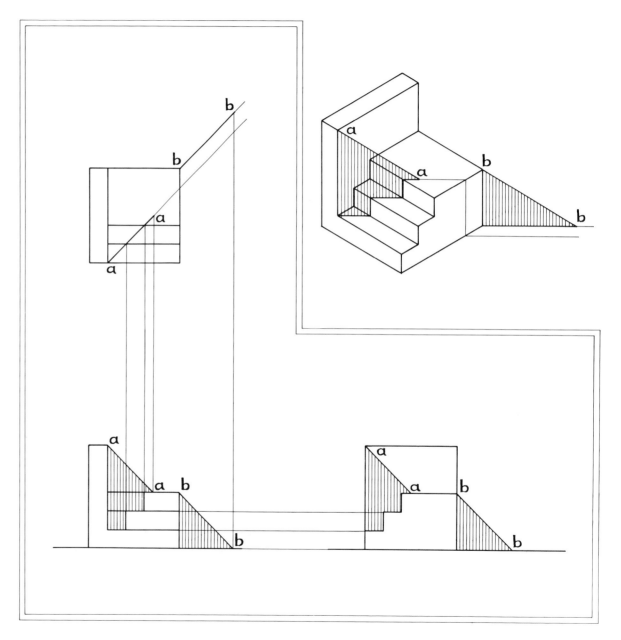

Figure 218. *Casting the shadow of a point.*

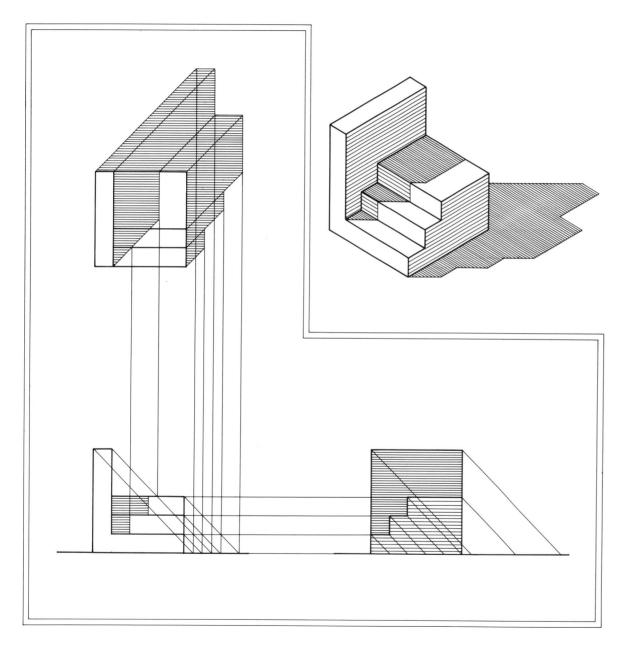

Casting the shadow of a solid To cast the shadow of a solid the shadows of the solid's several vertices are found via the slicing method and then connected.

Figure 219. *Casting the shadow of a solid.*

Shade and Shadow Orthographic Projection Exercises

Figure 220.

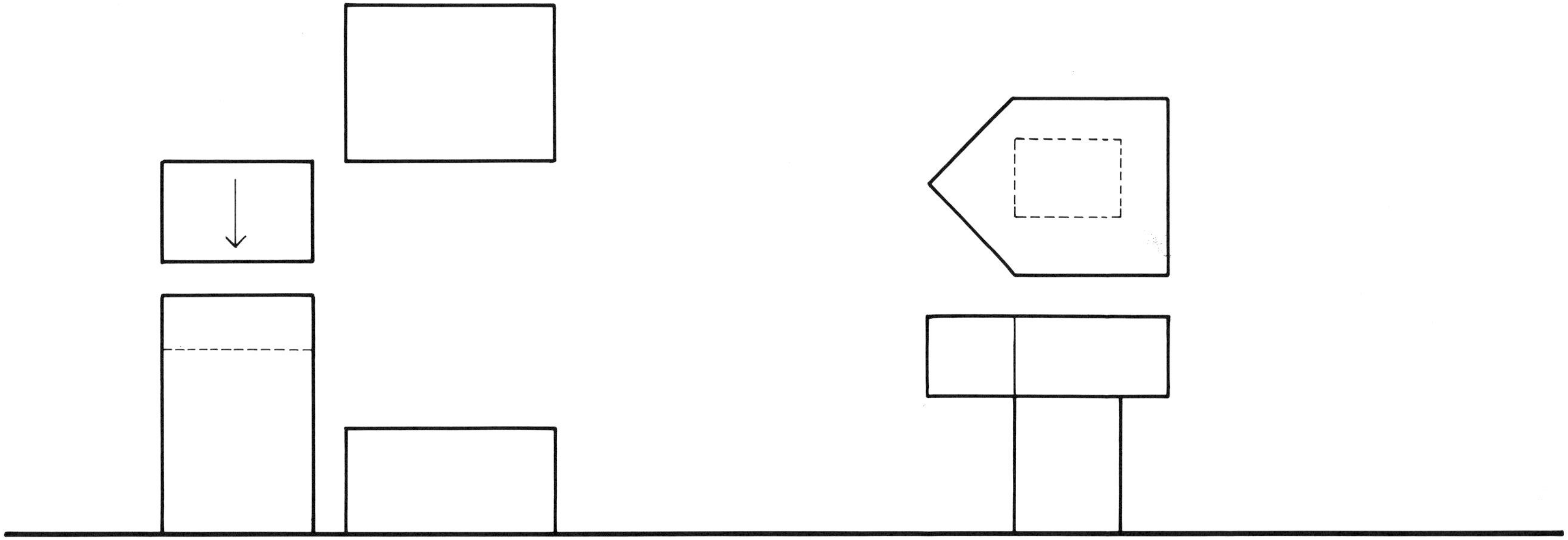

**Shade and Shadow
Orthographic Projection
Exercises** (Solutions)
Figure 221.

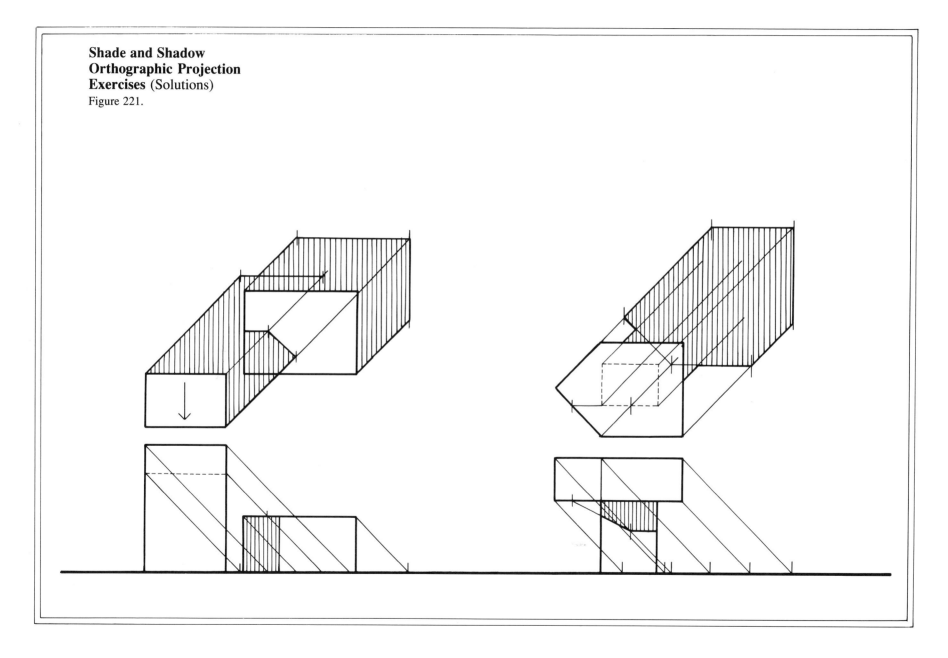

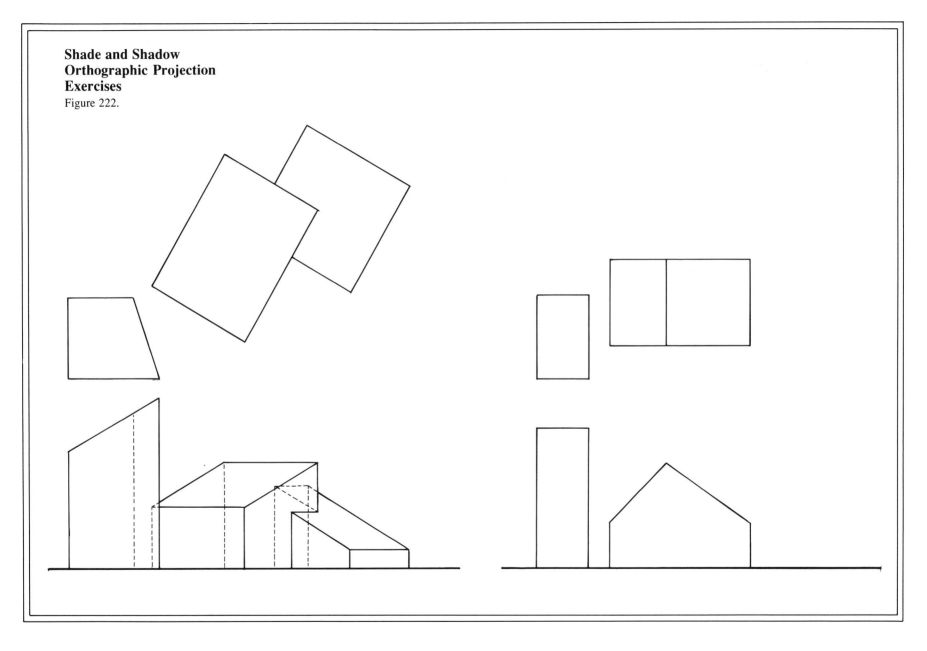

204

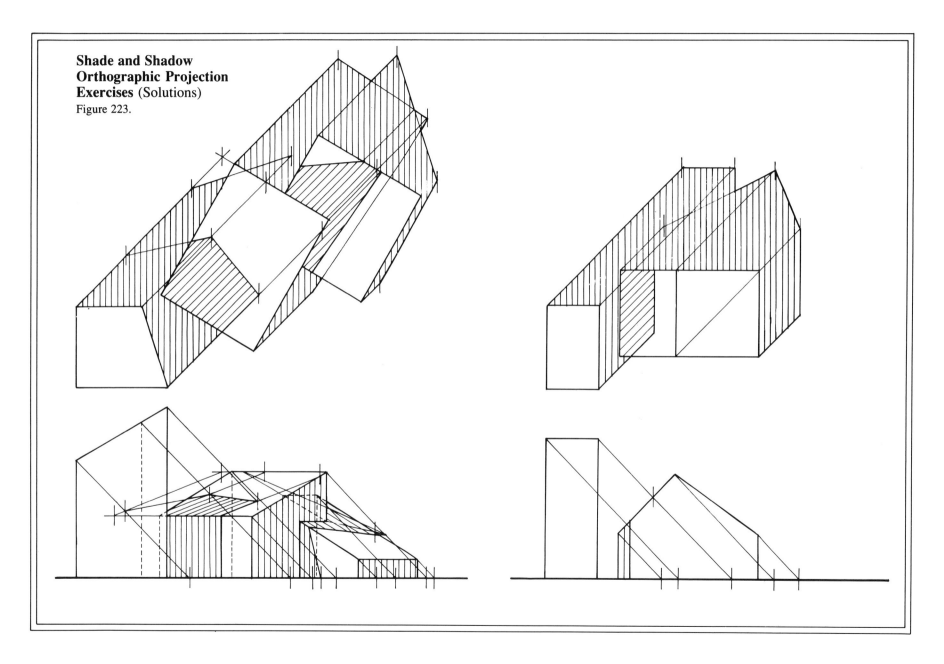

**Shade and Shadow
Orthographic Projection
Exercises** (Solutions)
Figure 223.

205

Glossary

Accommodation. Depth cue conditioned on the eye's changing focal length in viewing objects at various distances. Effective at close range only.

Aerial perspective. Depth cue conditioned on the effect of air on the color and visual acuity of objects at various distances from the observer.

Axonometric projection. System of projection including isometry and dimetry. Objects are positioned in an attitude tilted to the picture plane and projected to the picture plane with orthogonal (lines at 90°) sight lines. Axonometric views are drawn to scale, represent all three faces of a rectangular object (front, top, and side), and show parallel lines as parallel.

Bird's-eye view. Steeply inclined downward looking perspective view. Bird's-eye views yield a strong sense of the plan of an object or scene.

Center of vision. In perspective drawing, the point at which the viewer is looking on the picture plane.

Chiaroscuro. From the Italian *chiarro,* meaning light and *oscuro,* meaning dark, a technique of drawing which represents a full range of value from light to dark typically on a gray background.

Cone of vision. In perspective drawing, a conical field of vision radiating out from the viewer's eyes. Equivalent to the term breadth of field as it would be understood by a photographer. Typical cones of vision used in perspective range from 30° to 60° and rarely exceed 90°.

Contour. Lines on the surfaces of objects generated by profiles, interior edges, and surface textures.

Convergence. 1. Depth cue conditioned on the angle at which the two eyes must converge in viewing an object in close proximity to the viewer. **2.** In perspective drawing, the phenomenon of parallel lines appearing to come together at common vanishing points.

Depth cues. Conditions in the visual field that yield a perception of depth. Depth cues are generally divided in two groups: primary cues which are conditioned on the existence of two eyes, and secondary cues which are independent of the existence of two eyes.

Dimetric projection. A type of axonometric projection in which two of an object's spatial axes describe equal angles relative to the picture plane.

Disparity vision. Depth cue conditioned on the disparity between the views from the two eyes in viewing objects in close proximity to the viewer.

Drawing as making. A term used throughout this volume to characterize and refine a view that drawing is an investigatory process. This view considers a provisional belief in the real presence of objects on the page to be a significant point of departure for any drawing. Likewise, this view rejects understandings of drawing that give primary emphasis to visualization alone.

Ecological psychology. An understanding of perception that emphasizes the contribution of the order implicit in the environment. The principal advocate of this position is James J. Gibson.

Elevation. A horizontally directed orthographic view of a vertical face of an object or space.

Empathy. Sharing the same emotions or sensations as another person. In this text empathy is understood to be transferable to inanimate things.

Foreshortening. The apparent reduction in size of elements on longitudinal surfaces (surfaces that are turned relative to the viewer) with greater distance from the observer.

Gestalt psychology. An understanding of perception that emphasizes the role of predisposing laws in the process of perception.

Gesture drawing. A type of rapid and flowing free-hand drawing (usually from the figure) that seeks to embody a holistic understanding of the structural resolution of the stance of a body or object.

Ground line. In perspective drawing, a line on the picture plane where the ground plane or assumed ground plane meets the picture plane.

Horizon line. In perspective projection, a line on the picture plane that is level to the ground, passes through the center of vision, and represents the height of the viewer's eyes. The horizon line of perspective construction also coincides with the optical position of the *horizon* as a perceptual fact of our everyday environment, e.g., the horizon where the ocean appears to meet the sky.

Isometric projection. From the Greek *iso,* meaning same, and *metron,* meaning measure. A type of axonometric projection in which all three of an object's spatial axes describe equal angles relative to the picture plane.

Magic method. A method for constructing one-point perspectives using elevations or sectional views. This method derives from Alberti's system from the mid-fifteenth century.

Motion parallax. Depth cue conditioned on differences between apparent optical motions of objects at various distances from an observer who is moving.

Office method. A method for constructing one- or two-point perspective views. This method calls for using scaled orthographic drawings (typically a plan and an elevation), locating vanishing points for major sets of parallel lines on an assumed picture plane, and sighting points on objects with sight lines converging at a station point.

One-point perspective. The characteristic perspective view resulting from viewing in a direction that is parallel to the major spatial axis of an object or space. One-point views can be accurately constructed using the magic method.

Orthographic projection. System of projection including plans, elevations, and sections. Objects are positioned in an attitude parallel to the picture plane and projected to the picture plane with orthogonal (lines at 90°) sight lines. Orthographic views are drawn to scale, show parallel lines as parallel, represent frontal surfaces without distortion of shape or proportion, and represent only one face of a rectangular object (front, top, or side).

Overlap. Depth cue conditioned on near objects overlapping distant objects.

Oblique projection. System of projection including plan oblique and elevation oblique views. Objects are positioned in an attitude parallel to the picture plane and projected to the picture plane with *oblique* (lines at angles other than 90°) sight lines. Oblique views are drawn to scale, show parallel lines as parallel, represent frontal surfaces without distortion of shape or proportion, and represent all three faces of a rectangular object (front, top, and side). See also Paraline views.

Paraline views. Not a system of projection itself but rather a category of projective systems. Paraline views include those systems such as axonometric and oblique projection that show all three faces of objects and at the same time maintain parallel lines as parallel.

Perception. The process of recognizing form within sensory data. As distinct from sensation, perception attaches interpretation to sensation.

Perspective, linear. 1. Depth cue conditioned on the apparent convergence of parallel lines with greater distance from the observer. **2.** Drawing system built on the convergent projection of parallel lines to common vanishing points and on the convergent projection of sight lines to a single station point, the position of the viewer.

Pictorial depth cues. Those depth cues that are independent of the existence of two eyes and can be represented on a two-dimensional plane.

Picture plane. A plane, analogous to a window, through which drawings are projected.

Plan. A vertically directed orthographic view of a top or bottom face of an object or space.

Primary depth cues. Depth cues that are dependent upon the existence of two eyes or upon sensations of muscular response. Primary depth cues include: 1) Accommadation. 2) Disparity vision. 3) Convergence.

Secondary depth cues. Depth cues that are independent of the existence of two eyes. Secondary depth cues include: 1) Upward position in the visual field. 2) Overlap. 3) Shade and shadow. 4) Size perspective. 5) Aerial perspective. 6) Linear perspective. 7) Motion parallax. Secondary depth cues can be easily replicated on a two-dimensional plane in the form of drawings, paintings, and films.

Section. A horizontally directed orthographic view into the inside of an object or space.

Sensation. Uninterpreted sensory stimulation, e.g., the retinal image as distinct from perceived space.

Shade and shadow. Depth cue predicated on the information provided by shade and shadow.

Sight line. A line used to project points on object to equivalent positions on a picture plane. Sight lines can vary in their attitude to the picture plane; in orthographic and axonometric projection, they are always orthogonals (at 90°); in oblique projection they are oblique (at angles other than 90°); in perspective projection they converge at a single point, the station point, the position of the viewer.

Size perspective. Depth cue conditioned on the apparent reduction in size of objects (of known size) with greater distance from the observer.

Slice line. In using the slicing method to cast shadows, the line formed by the intersection of the *slice* with the ground or object receiving the shadow. The shadows of individual points are found along the *slice line*.

Slicing method. In casting shadows in isometric, orthographic, and perspective projection, the method of locating the cast shadows of individual points by passing a vertical plane or *slice* through a point in an attitude parallel to the plane described by the convergence of the sun's rays with the ground.

Spatial armature. A geometric framework of coordinates on which a drawing can be constructed.

Station point. In perspective projection, the point representing the position of the viewer to which convergent sight lines are drawn.

Substitute. Descriptive noun used by E. H. Gombrich to denote the relationship that any representation has to the thing that it represents. According to Gombrich, representations derive their meaning from their capacity to take the place of their references within certain contexts.

Surface texture. Term used by James J. Gibson to mean any condition of surface that reflects light that varies from light to dark across its surface.

Three-point perspective. The characteristic perspective view resulting from viewing in a direction that is diagonal to all three major spatial axes of an object or space.

Textural gradient. Term used by James J. Gibson to mean the condition at the point of impact of light on the retina that corresponds in an ordinal manner (point for point) to the texture from which light has been reflected.

Transactional psychology or transactional empiricism. An understanding of perception that emphasizes the contributions of learning and interaction with the environment to the process of perceiving. Principal advocates of this position are John Dewey and Adelbert Ames.

Two-point perspective. The characteristic perspective view resulting from viewing in a direction that is diagonal to two major spatial axes of an object or space. Two-point views can be accurately constructed using the office method.

Upward position in visual field. Depth cue predicated on the tendency of objects to be seen against the background of a continuous ground or floor surface. Objects that are farther tend to be located higher in the visual field and those that are nearer tend to be located lower in the visual field.

Value. As distinct from hue, a measure of the lightness and darkness of a color or tone.

Vertical measuring line. In perspective drawing, a line on the picture plane used to generate vertical information at scale.

Vanishing point. In perspective projection, a point on the picture plane at which a set of parallel lines appears to converge.

Visual field. The sensation of vision projected on the retina. See visual world.

Visual world. Term used by James J. Gibson to distinguish the boundless character of visual perception from the bounded character of the visual field. The visual world encompasses all that might be seen if the viewer is allowed to move. The visual field refers to the sensation of one moment of seeing, i.e., the retinal image.

Bibliography

Allport, Floyd H. *Theories of Perception and the Concept of Structure.* New York: John Wiley & Sons, Inc., 1955.
Provides an overview of the process of perceiving as well as in-depth discussion of various points of view including gestalt psychology and transactional psychology.

Arnheim, R. *Art and Visual Perception.* new version. Berkley and Los Angeles: University of California Press, 1974.
Arnheim's central work considers the perception and representation of shape, form, and space from the perspective of gestalt psychology. Includes analysis of the development of drawings by children.

————— .*Visual Thinking.* Berkley and Los Angeles: University of California Press, 1969.
More wide-ranging in its scope than *Art and Visual Perception.* Considers visual perception as a cognitive activity that is both separate from and related to other modes of thought.

————— .*"Gestalt Psychology and Artistic Form"* in *Aspects of Form.* Edited by L.L. Whyte. Bloomington: Indiana University Press, 1966, pp. 196-208.

Barnett, H. G. *Innovation: the Basis of Cultural Change.* New York: McGraw Hill, 1953.
Account of the dynamics of perception during the process of design from the general perspective of gestalt psychology. Appendix, "On Things," provides an excellent account of the perception of qualities of things.

Blanshard, Francis Bradshaw. *Retreat from Likeness in the Theory of Painting.* New York: Columbia University Press, 1949.
Provides a brief account from several points of view of the role of appearance in making pictorial art. Includes summaries of the positions of Plato, Aristotle, Reynolds, Plotinus, and Shopenhauer.

Boring, E. G. *Sensation and Perception in the History of Experimental Psychology.* New York: Appleton, 1942.
Provides an historical account of changing understandings of perception and changing interpretations of specific phenomena including the primary and secondary depth cues.

Cooper, Douglas. Drawing and Perceiving, Silver Spring: Information Dynamics, 1983.
Earliest version of this volume.

————— . "Drawings as Substitute Places," in *Dichotomy.* Edited by G. Dodds. Detroit: University of Detroit School of Architecture, 1983, pp. 76-83.
Earlier version of chapter 3 in this volume.

————— . "Drawing, Touching and Moving," in *Journal of Architectural Education.* volume XXXV n 3, Spring 1982, pp. 9–13.
Presents the early experiments in applying Nicholaides's figure-drawing exercises to drawings of architectural subjects.

————— . "Miniature Substitutes," in Representation and Architecture. Edited by Omer Akin and Eleanor Weinel. Silver Spring: Information Dynamics, 1982, pp. 185–189.
Earlier version of preface to chapter 4 in this volume.

————— . "Talking/Drawing/Moving," unpublished paper.
Proposed that childhood drawing up until the age of seven years is part of a hybrid and mutually complimentary form of representation that includes talking and gesturing. The drawing is understood as giving presence, the talking as giving voice and qualification, and the gesturing as giving demonstration and enactment.

Deregowski, J. B. "Pictorial Perception and Culture" in *Readings from Scientific American.* Edited by R. Held. San Francisco: W. H. Freeman Co., 1971, pp. 79-85.
Based on studies of Zulu tribesmen, presents evidence that visual perception and specifically linear perspective are culturally based.

Dewey, John. *Art as Experience*. New York: Minton, Balch & Company, 1934.

    A view of art presented by one of the central figures within the transactionalist point of view.

Edgarton, S. Y. *The Renaissance Rediscovery of Linear Perspective*. New York: Basic Books, 1975.

    Provocative and wide-ranging book that relates the rediscovery of linear perspective at the onset of the 1400s to developments in other fields including the arrival in Florence of a copy of Ptolemy's World Atlas, Columbus's voyage to America, and an overall changing world view. Book includes a detailed account of Brunelleschi's perspective experiments conducted in front of the Baptistery in Florence.

Edwards, Betty. *Drawing on the Right Side of the Brain*. New York: St. Martins Press, 1979.

    Presents a drawing pedagogy based on the model put forth by R. W. Sperry which proposed that spatial reasoning is a function of the right hemisphere of the brain and that verbal reasoning is a function of the left.

Gardner, Howard. *Art Mind and Body*. New York: Basic Books, Inc., 1982.

    By one of the central figures in Harvard's *Project Zero*, focuses on the artistic development of young children. Includes discussion of the noted child prodigy, Nadia and, as part of a general discussion of her case, takes a critical view of positions that have explained her case on the basis of a right-brain left-brain split of functions. Discussion of children's art is preceded by a lengthy presentation of several points of view on the correctness of any developmental model. Views of Jean Piaget, Naom Chomsky, Claude Lévi-Strauss, and Ernst Cassirer are discussed.

Gibson, J. J. *The Perception of the Visual World*. Boston: Houghton Mifflin, 1950.

    Gibson's first major work and the foundation for much of the second chapter of this volume. Though he would modify and expand his position in his later work (this work concentrates on the retinal image), this book lays the groundwork for Gibson's radical view that the environment provides sensory data that is in itself already ordered.

———. *The Senses Considered as Perceptual Systems*. Boston: Houghton Mifflin, 1966.

    Provides significant modification and breadth to his earlier work, *The Perception of the Visual World*. Here he gives greater emphasis to the role of both kinesthetic interaction with the environment and the interaction of the senses with each other.

———. *The Ecological Approach to Visual Perception*. Boston: Houghton Mifflin, 1979.

    Gibson's concluding work in which he returns to his original focus on visual perception. Study of the role of movement as a constant condition of the observer is used to present the ambient optical array as a sufficient condition for vision.

Gombrich, E. H. *Art and Illusion*. Princeton: Princeton University Press, 1960.

    Gombrich's powerful study that considers pictorial representation from the multiple perspectives current in modern psychology. Gombrich draws significantly from gestalt psychology, and transactional empiricism, as well as from the formative work of J. J. Gibson.

———. *The Image and the Eye*. Ithaca: Cornell University Press, 1982.

    Gombrich continues the direction of his earlier work, *Art and Illusion*, but in this volume builds more significantly on the mature work of J. J. Gibson.

———. "Meditations on a Hobby Horse" in *Aspects of Form*, Edited by L.L. Whyte. Bloomington: Indiana University Press, 1966, pp. 209-228.

    Gombrich's oft-cited parable on the mechanisms of representation. This work is key to the formulation of drawing as an act of making that is presented in the third chapter of this volume.

Gregory, R. L. *Eye and Brain*. 3d ed. New York: McGraw Hill, 1978.

    Readable volume introducing the broad issues of visual perception. Includes discussion of the physiology of seeing and explanations from various points of view of noted visual illusions and linear perspective.

Haldane, J. B. S. "On Being the Right Size," in *World of Mathematics*. New York: Simon and Schuster, 1956, Vol. 2, pp. 952-957.

Harwood, A. C. *The Recovery of Man in Childhood*. Spring Valley, N.Y.: Anthroposophic Press, 1958.

    Provides an excellent discussion of the relationship of Steiner's pedagogy to Goethe and a year by year overview of the Waldorf School curriculum.

Highlands, Delbert. "Translation," in Representation and Architecture. Edited by Omer Akin and Eleanor Weinel. Silver Spring: Information Dynamics, 1982, pp. 237–243.

Hillman, Hans. Illustrations in *Fliegen Papier*. (*Fliegenpapier* is the German translation of Dashiell Hammett's *Fly Paper*) Frankfurt am Main: Zweitausendeins, 1982.

    Ink wash drawings that are instructive on the use of shade and shadow as an issue of composition and light-dark contrast

Ittleson, W. *The Ames Demonstrations in Perception*. Princeton: Princeton University Press, 1952.

    Documents the noted demonstrations of Adelbert Ames Jr. that have provided significant support for the transactional position.

Koffka, Kurt. *Principles of Gestalt Psychology*. New York: Harcourt Brace & Co., 1935.

Lorenz, Konrad. "The Role of Gestalt Perception in Animal and Human Behavior" in *Aspects of Form*. Edited by L.L. Whyte. Bloomington: Indiana University Press, 1966, pp. 157-178.

Excellent account of the mechanism of perception as understood from the perspective of gestalt psychology.

Lynch, Kevin. *The Image of the City.* Cambridge: MIT Press, 1960.
I sense there is a relationship between what is proposed in chapter 3 of this volume and some of the drawings some have done predicated on Lynch's work.

Maxwell G. Mayo. *Line and Light* . Pittsburgh: Department of Architecture, Carnegie Mellon University, 1971) Chapters 1-9.
Background for shade and shadow in isometric and orthographic projection as presented in this volume.

McKim, Robert H. *Experiences in Visual Thinking.* Monterey: Brooks/Cole Co., 1972.
Addresses representation and its relationship to creativity and design process.

Pirenne, M. H. *Optics, Painting and Photography.* Cambridge: Cambridge University Press, 1970.
Optics of both the generation and viewing of perspective drawings. Limitations of perspective as a representation of the visual field are addressed. Includes a description of projective procedures used in executing the ceiling fresco at S. Ignazio by the Pozzo family.

Panofsky, Erwin. "Die Perspektive als Symbolische Form" in *Vorträge der Bibliothek, Warburg. 1924-25* Berlin-Leipzig: 1925, pp.258-330.
Influential paper that presents a critique of perspective on optical and artistic grounds. As for the latter, it considers its limitations both from the well known position of Plato (ie. perspective distorts reality) and from his own position: perspective objectifies subjective reality. Panofsky also identifies a paradox of perspective particularly as it devel-

ops in Northern Europe; while, on the one hand, it closes pictures from a role as a vehicle of religious symbolic order, it also opens a new role, within the Baroque, as a vehicle of religious vision.

Piaget, Jean. *The Child's Conception of the World.* London: Granada Publishing, 1973.

———— and Inhelder, Bärbel. *The Child's Conception of Space.* New York: W. W. Norton, 1948.

Rylander, Mark. "The Importance of Perspective in the Design Process," in *Crit XV.* Edited by Laura Todd. Washington, D.C.: American Institute of Architecture Students, Inc., 1985.
Presents Philip Grausman's drawing course at Yale University. My own understanding of the *spatial armature* owes to my contact with a former student of that course, my colleague at Carnegie Mellon, Bruce Lindsey.

Spock, Marjorie. *Teaching as a Lively Art.* Spring Valley, N.Y.: The Anthroposophic Press, 1978.
Readable account of Rudolf Steiner education (including painting and drawing) from kindergarten through the eighth grade. Rich with personal accounts by the author.

Segal et al. *The Influence of Culture on Visual Perception.* New York: Bobbs Merril Co., 1966.
Looks at visual perception (including well known visual illusions) from the stance of cultural relativism.

Stockmeyer, Karl E. A. *Rudolf Steiner's Curriculum for Waldorf Schools.* Dornach: Rudolf Steiner Verlag, 1965.
Edited compilation from Steiner's own writing of a year by year description of and argument for his curriculum.

Warren, Richard M. and Roslyn P. *Helmholtz on Perception.*

New York: John Wiley, 1968.
Presents a brief history of the key nineteenth century empiricist and forerunner of present day transactional empiricism, Hermann L. F. Helmholtz. Includes original treatises of Helmholtz on questions of visual perception together with commentary by the authors on each.

White, John. *The Birth and Rebirth of Pictorial Space.* Boston: Boston Book and Art Shop, 1967.
Addresses pictorial space at the critical juncture before and after Brunelleschi's perspective demonstration. Includes discussion of the work of Cimabue, Giotto, Masaccio, Donatello, Ghiberti, Paolo Uccello, and the Sienese masters. It concludes with a brief look back at the pictorial space of imperial Rome, in particular the frescoes of Pompeii.

Winner, Ellen. *Invented Worlds.* Camridge: Harvard University Press, 1982.
Along with Howard Gardner one of the central figures in Harvard's *Project Zero.* Book provides a good overview of psychological issues as they relate to the arts. Particularly strong in its explanations of children's art.

Wright, L. *Perspective in Perspective.* London: Routledge & Kegan Paul, 1983.
In depth account of the history and techniques of perspective from the Greeks and Romans to the present day. Provides detailed accounts of Alberti's method of generating perspectives with distance points, Piero della Francesca and Paolo Uccello's generation of perspectives from plans, and the Pozzo family's technique for projecting the ceiling fresco at S. Ignazio in Rome.

Yates, Francis A. *The Art of Memory.* Chicago: University of Chicago Press, 1966.
Discussion of the method of loci for memory.

Index